The Hidden Messages in Water

The Hidden Messages in Water

Masaru Emoto

Translated by
David A. Thayne

BEYOND
WORDS
Publishing
I N C

Beyond Words Publishing, Inc.
20827 N.W. Cornell Road, Suite 500
Hillsboro, Oregon 97124-9808
503-531-8700

Copyright © 2004 by Beyond Words Publishing
Translated by David A. Thayne

Originally published as "MIZU WA KOTAE WO SHITTEIRU" by
Masaru Emoto.

Original Japanese edition published by Sunmark Publishing, Inc.,
Tokyo, Japan.
Copyright © 2001 by Masaru Emoto.

English translation rights arranged with Sunmark Publishing, Inc.,
Tokyo through InterRights, Inc., Tokyo.

Managing editor: Beth Caldwell Hoyt
Copyeditor/Proofreader: David Abel
Design: Jerry Soga
Composition: William H. Brunson Typography Services

Printed in Korea

Distributed to the book trade by Publishers Group West

Library of Congress Cataloging-in-Publication Data

Emoto, Masaru, 1943–
    [Mizu wa kotae o shitte iru. English]
    The hidden messages in water / Emoto Masaru.
        p.   cm.
    ISBN 1-58270-114-8
    1. Water—Philosophy.   2. Water quality.   3. Anthroposophy.
    I. Title.

RA591.5.E4613   2004
613—dc22

                                                    2004002415

The corporate mission of Beyond Words Publishing, Inc.:
Inspire to Integrity

In memory of my maternal grandfather,
aunts, and uncles

TABLE OF CONTENTS

INTRODUCTION

More than ten years have passed since I began taking photographs of frozen ice crystals.

For years before that I had conducted research into the measurement of wave fluctuations in water, but when I started learning about crystals, I discovered that water expresses itself in a vast variety of ways.

I learned that these photographs of crystals are filled with much wisdom for us. In contrast to tap water, natural water displays a beautiful array of crystals—even more so when the natural water is exposed to beautiful music. There are also fascinating differences generated in the crystals when the water is shown different words, such as "gratitude" or "stupid." These crystals are filled with lessons concerning how we should—and must—live our lives.

In June 1999, I published a collection of photographs in a book called *The Messages of Water* from a small publishing company that I called Hado Kyoikusha (Wave Fluctuation Publishing). Although this book was self-published and not intended to be sold in the large bookstores, word of mouth resulted in it becoming a bestseller.

This is something that almost never happens in the publishing industry. I was filled half with amazement as this was happening right in front of my eyes, and half with appreciation for the many people who took the time to tell others about the book.

In order to share my book with more people, I had all the Japanese explanations translated for an English version. This led to further successes, and I began receiving requests from Switzerland and other countries throughout the world to give lectures.

The publishing of these crystal photographs, with the many messages that they have for the world, couldn't have come at a more appropriate moment in history, and it may well be a sign of the times that so many people are receptive of these messages. I thank God that I have been given the opportunity to work in this capacity.

I understand that some people have difficulty with the word or concept *God*. The main focus in this book is water. And the more you understand water, the more difficult you will find it to deny the existence of a god. I'd like you to think about your feelings on this topic as you look through the crystal photographs found herein.

When I was first asked to write this book for Sunmark Publishing in Japan, I immediately knew that there were many marvelous things inside me that I wanted to write about, and when I told this to Nobutaka Ueki, President of Sunmark Publishing, he said that was what he wanted me to focus on. He even sent along a subordinate, Ryuya Saitou, to hear my lectures in Switzerland.

Now that the book is finished, I am filled with a sense of satisfaction. This book has given me a "stage" from which to speak to you about the "fluctuation" theories that I have studied for more than a decade, and also about my own experiences, my research based on the observation of human behavior, and my own thoughts concerning the cosmos.

I wish to take this opportunity to expression my appreciation to Shinji Tanigawa, president of Kokoro Inc.; Naoki Uchiki, Chief Editor of Sunmark; Tatsuya Saito; and also to the people who I interviewed for this book.

I also owe appreciation to Tetsuya Taguchi, past president of Nichirei Ice Inc., who provided much of the water that I used to make the crystals introduced in this book.

Thank you to Beyond Words Publishing for publishing this book in English, so that more people around the world can read about our relationship with water.

I must not forget to offer my gratitude to all the readers of this book. And, finally, I must say thank you and pay my respects to the water of the cosmos.

Thank you.

As you begin reading this book, I'd like to ask you to evaluate your life. More specifically, I'd like you to ask yourself if you are happy.

Of course, your definition of happiness will depend upon who you are—but do you have a sense of peace in your heart, a feeling of security about your future, and a feeling of anticipation when you wake up in the morning? If we can call this happiness, then would you say that at this moment you are happy?

I think I can safely say that not many people will be able to reply with a resounding yes. Most people are unable to say that their life is everything they had hoped it would be. What is it that causes us so much pain? What is going on in the world that prevents so many people from simply being happy?

It seems to me that we are living in an age of chaos. Chaos describes a condition of confusion, indicative of the unorganized matter that existed before the creation of the cosmos.

Simply by going about our lives, we find ourselves worn out and fatigued. Newspapers and television bombard us with information, and at work we face problems and misunderstandings. The sources of our problems seem numerous and overwhelming.

This is likely to be a fact of life no matter where in the world we go. This tiny planet of ours is covered with economic conflict, domestic discord, ethnic prejudice, environmental distress, religious wars, and every other type of problem imaginable. And all the bad news about people suffering, people enjoying the suffering, people getting richer, people getting poorer, the oppressed and the oppressors, reaches us within a matter of seconds from the opposite side of the globe.

Who, might we ask, is responsible for all this suffering? The world is becoming an ever more divided, estranged, and complicated place to live. We are already up to our necks in chaos, but the world's troubles seem to be getting deeper and deeper.

One thing we all have in common is that we are looking for a way out. Everyone is looking for an answer—and it is an answer so simple and effective that it has heretofore eluded us.

~~~~~~

So what is the cause of all this chaos? What is at the center of it all? Whatever it is, it is pushing the world away from harmony and towards discord.

Perhaps this is an inevitable phenomenon. Though we all belong to the same species, if we live in different places and in different skin ways, the way we think is bound to be different.

And to make matters worse, most people have difficulty accepting things that are unlike the things around them. The result is a neverending process of troubles and suffering. It would seem that as long as people are people, any solution proposed is certain to come up short.

And so now we are back where we started. Can there ever be a single solution that can apply to all people on the globe, that everyone can be convinced of, and that is so simple that everyone can understand it?

In fact, I have found the answer, and it is just this: The average human body is 70 percent water.

We start out life being 99 percent water, as fetuses. When we are born, we are 90 percent water, and by the time we reach adulthood we are down to 70 percent. If we die of old age, we will probably be about 50 percent water. In other words, throughout our lives *we exist mostly as water*.

From a physical perspective, humans are water. When I realized this and started to look at the world from this perspective, I began to see things in a whole new way.

First, I realized that this connection to water applies to all peoples. Therefore, what I am about to say applies to everyone, all over the world.

I believe I am also starting to see the way that people should live their lives. So how can people live happy and healthy lives? The answer is to purify the water that makes up 70 percent of your body.

Water in a river remains pure because it is moving. When water becomes trapped, it dies. Therefore, water must constantly be circulated. The water—or blood—in the bodies of the sick is usually stagnant. When blood stops flowing, the body starts to decay, and if the blood in your brain stops, it can be life threatening.

But why does blood become stagnant? We can see this condition as the stagnation of the emotions. Modern researchers have shown that the condition of the mind has a direct impact on the condition of the body. When you are living a full and enjoyable life, you feel better physically, and when your life is filled with struggles and sorrow, your body knows it.

So when your emotions flow throughout your body, you feel a sense of joy and you move towards physical health.

Moving, changing, flowing—this is what life is all about.

~~~~~~

If we consider that before we became human beings, we existed as water, we get closer to finding the answer to the basic question of what a human being is. If we have a clear understanding of water, we will better understand the human body, and even unlock the mystery of why we were born and exist as we do.

So just what is water? Your first answer might be that it is a life force. If we lose 50 percent of the water in our bodies, we can no longer maintain life. Water, carried by blood and bodily fluids, is the means by which nourishment is circulated throughout our bodies. This flow of water enables us to live active lives. Water serves as the transporter of energy throughout our body.

This transport of energy is similar to a freight car that moves throughout the body. If the body is clogged and soiled, then the cargo in the freight car will also become filthy, and so it is essential that water always remain clean.

More now than in the past, the medical community has begun to see water as a transporter of energy, and it is even being used in the treatment of illness. Homeopathy is one such field where the value of water is recognized.

Homeopathy originated in Germany in the first half of the nineteenth century with the work of Samuel Hahnemann (1791–1843), but its roots go back to the father of medicine, Hippocrates (c. 460–c. 370 BC), who wrote down many treatments similar to those promoted by homeopathy. In a word, these pioneers of medicine taught us to "treat like with like, fight poison with poison."

For example, if someone is suffering from lead poisoning, symptoms can be alleviated by drinking water with the minutest amount of lead in it—an amount ranging 1 part in 10^{12} (one trillion) to 1 part in 10^{400}!

At this level, the matter no longer for practical purposes remains in the water, but the *characteristics* of the matter do remain, and this forms the medicine for treating lead poisoning.

Homeopathy proposes that the greater the dilution, the greater the effectiveness. The logical conclusion is that the denser the poison in the body, the higher should be the dilution ratio.

Another way to express this idea is that, instead of the *effect* of the matter being used to get rid of the symptoms, the information *copied* to the water is being used to cancel out the information of the symptoms from the poison.

So water has the ability to *copy* and *memorize* information. We may also say that the water of the oceans has memories of the creatures that live in the ocean. The earth's glaciers may well contain millions of years of the planet's history.

Water circulates around the globe, flowing through our bodies and spreading to the rest of the world. If we were capable of reading this information contained in the memory of water, we would read a story of epic proportions.

To understand water is to understand the cosmos, the marvels of nature, and life itself.

~~~~~~

I have studied water for many years. The realization that water has the ability to copy information has changed my life. After making this discovery in America, I brought it back with me to Japan, and have since used the information-copying function of water to help people recover their health.

At that time, however, doctors would not even consider the possibility that water by itself had healing capabilities. I was and am fully convinced that water is able to memorize and transport information, but this suggestion has been met with complete rejection by the medical community.

In 1988, the French scientist Jacques Benveniste undertook an experiment to test the basic principles of homeopathy. He diluted a medicine with water to the point where the medicine was no longer detectable by clinical means, and then he discovered that this dilution had the same effect on patients as the undiluted medicine.

A year after he submitted his results to the British scientific journal *Nature*, they were finally published, along with the comment that the results of the experiment were doubtful and without any physical proof. The hypothesis has remained buried and forgotten ever since.

Whenever someone comes along with research and experiments that turn the scientific community on its ear, the reaction, to one degree or another, is usually the same. I long wondered if it might be possible to find physical evidence of the ability of water to memorize information—might there be some way of seeing it with the physical eye?

When your heart is open to possibilities, you start to notice small things that can lead to enormous discoveries. And one day I casually opened a book to words that jumped off the page: "No two snow crystals are exactly the same."

Of course, I had learned this same thing in elementary school. The faces of all the snowflakes that have fallen on the earth for millions of years have all been different. However, I read this sentence as if it had a completely different meaning because my heart was open and receptive to its message. The next moment I thought, *If I freeze water and look at the crystals, each one will look totally unique*. And that moment marked my first step on an adventure into a new and unexplored world. My plan was to freeze water and take pictures of the crystals.

It's my nature not to want to sit on a fresh idea. I immediately asked a young researcher in my company to start experimenting, but this was a field that no one knew anything about. There was nothing to assure us that our efforts would eventually pay off. Oddly enough, I never doubted that they would. I knew with certainty that my hypothesis was correct and that the experiments would go well—*I just knew it*. I usually suffer from a critical shortage of perseverance, but this time I refused to give up.

My first step was to lease an extremely accurate microscope and look at water frozen in a kitchen refrigerator. However, since the photographs were taken at room temperature, the ice would soon melt. It took us quite some time before we were able to get any photographs of crystals.

Late each evening, I would take the young researcher to dinner and try to encourage him. I told him that I only expected him to do his best.

After two months of experiments, we finally succeeded in getting one photograph. The water gave us a photograph of a beautiful hexagonal crystal. I was filled with excitement when the researcher came to me with the news.

I now have a large walk-in refrigerator where the temperature is maintained at $-5°C$ ($23°F$) for experimenting, but it all started with that first photograph.

Considering the method we used and what I know now, it was quite miraculous that we were able to get that first photograph at all.

What you really know is possible in your heart is possible. We make it possible by our will. What we imagine in our minds becomes our world. That's just one of many things that I have learned from water.

~~~~~~

The crystal photographs that I started taking proved to be extremely eloquent in expressing the world. I found within them a profound philosophy. Crystals emerge for only twenty or thirty seconds as the temperature rises and the ice starts to melt. The truths of the cosmos take shape and become visible, if only for a few moments. This short window of time gives us a glimpse into a world that is indeed magical.

Let me explain how I go about taking photographs of crystals.

I put fifty different types of water in fifty different Petri dishes. (I used one hundred during the first few years.) I then freeze the dishes at −20°C (−4°F) for three hours in a freezer. The result is that surface tension forms drops of ice in the Petri dishes about one millimeter across. The crystal appears when you shine a light on the crown of the drop of ice.

Of course, the result is never fifty similar crystals, and sometimes no crystals at all are formed. When we graphed the formation of the crystals, we realized that different water formed different crystals. Some of them were clearly similar, some were deformed, and in some types of water, no crystals at all formed.

First I looked at the crystals of tap water from different locations. The water of Tokyo was a disaster—not a single complete crystal was formed. Tap water includes a dose of chlorine used to sanitize it, utterly destroying the structure found in natural water.

However, within natural water, no matter where it came from—natural springs, underground rivers, glaciers, and the upper reaches of rivers—complete crystals formed.

My efforts to photograph ice crystals and conduct research began to move ahead. Then one day the researcher—who was as caught up in the project as I—said something completely out of left field: "Let's see what happens when we expose the water to music."

I knew that it was possible for the vibrations of music to have an effect on the water. I myself enjoy music immensely, and had even had hopes of becoming a professional musician as a child, and so I was all in favor of this off-the-wall experiment.

At first we had no idea what music we would use and under what conditions we would conduct the experiment. But after considerable trial and error, we reached the conclusion that the best method was probably the simplest—put a bottle of water on a table between two speakers and expose it to a volume at which a person might normally listen to music. We would also need to use the same water that we had used in previous experiments.

We first tried distilled water from a drugstore.

The results astounded us. Beethoven's Pastoral Symphony, with its bright and clear tones, resulted in beautiful and well-formed crystals. Mozart's 40th Symphony, a graceful prayer to beauty, created crystals that were delicate and elegant. And the crystals formed by exposure to Chopin's Etude in E, Op. 10, No. 3, surprised us with their lovely detail.

All the classical music that we exposed the water to resulted in well-formed crystals with distinct characteristics. In contrast, the water exposed to violent heavy-metal music resulted in fragmented and malformed crystals at best.

But our experimenting didn't stop there. We next thought about what would happen if we wrote words or phrases like "Thank you" and "Fool" on pieces of paper, and wrapped the paper around the bottles of water with the words facing in. It didn't seem logical for water to "read" the writing, understand the meaning, and change its form accordingly. But I knew from the experiment with music that strange things could happen. We felt as if we were explorers setting out on a journey through an unmapped jungle.

The results of the experiments didn't disappoint us. Water exposed to "Thank you" formed beautiful hexagonal crystals, but water exposed to the word "Fool" produced crystals similar to the water exposed to heavy-metal music, malformed and fragmented.

Further experimenting showed that water exposed to positive expressions like "Let's do it!" created attractive, well-formed crystals, but that water exposed to negative expressions like "Do it!" barely formed any crystals at all.

The lesson that we can learn from this experiment has to do with the power of words. The vibration of good words has a positive effect on our world, whereas the vibration from negative words has the power to destroy.

~~~~~~

Learning about water is like an exploration to discover how the cosmos works, and the crystals revealed through water are like the portal into another dimension. As we continued with our experiments in taking photographs of crystals, we found that we were setting out to climb the stairs toward an understanding of the profound truths of the cosmos.

I particularly remember one photograph. It was the most beautiful and delicate crystal that I had so far seen—formed by being exposed to the words "love and gratitude." It was if the water had rejoiced and celebrated by creating a flower in bloom. It was so beautiful that I can say that it actually changed my life from that moment on.

Water had taught me the delicacy of the human soul, and the impact that "love and gratitude" can have on the world.

In Japan, it is said that words of the soul reside in a spirit called *kotodama* or the *spirit of words*, and the act of speaking words has the power to change the world. We all know that words have an enormous influence on the way we think and feel, and that things generally go more smoothly when positive words are used. However, up until now we have never been able to physically see the effect of positive words.

Words are an expression of the soul. And the condition of our soul is very likely to have an enormous impact on the water that composes as much as 70 percent of our body, and this impact will in no small way affect our bodies. People who are in good health are also generally in good spirits. Indeed, a healthy spirit most comfortably resides in a healthy body.

Out of desire to help as many people as possible remain or become healthy, I had worked for years taking care of the sick. And the more afflicted people that I see, the more I become convinced that illness is not just an individual problem, but a result of the deformation of society as a whole.

Unless something is done about the deformed world that we live in, and unless we can heal the wounded soul, the number of people suffering from physical illnesses will not decline.

So what are the deformities of the world? These are the deformities of the soul, and such deformities have an impact on the cosmos itself. Just as a drop in a pond creates a ripple that spreads out endlessly, the deformity of even one soul spreads throughout the world, resulting in global deformities.

But all is not lost—there is hope. There is salvation, and it's called "love and gratitude."

The earth is searching. It wants to be beautiful. It wants to be the most beautiful that it can be. Earlier I said that we could define the human being as water. I am quite certain that the water in the people who look at the photographs of crystals undergoes some form of change.

And I have found the most beautiful crystal of all— the one created by "love and gratitude." This is supposedly what all the world's religions are founded on, and if that were true, there would be no need for laws. You already know the answer. "Love and gratitude" are the words that must serve as the guide for the world.

Water teaches in a very clear way how we must live our lives. The story of water reaches from every individual cell to encompass the entire cosmos. I hope that you will feel the same anticipation and excitement that I felt as I discovered the unfolding of this drama.

CHAPTER ONE

Of What Is the Universe Made?

Understanding the fact that we are essentially water is the key to uncovering the mysteries of the universe. If you reexamine the world around you from this new perspective, you will start to see things as you have never seen them before.

The various events that unfold throughout a person's life are events reflected in water. The individual and society make up one enormous ocean; by adding our individual drops to this ocean, we participate in the formation of society.

I wanted as many people as possible to hear the message that water has for us, and so I decided to publish the photographs of the ice crystals. This act was only a small drop, but it created a ripple that resulted in an ever-expanding wave that has had enormous impact on my life, and the lives of many others.

I first published my photographs in 1999, six long years after I started out on this unusual venture. During those first six years, a mountain of photographs had accumulated and was just sitting there in my office.

To prepare the photographs for publication, I tried to put them in some sort of order, and as I did so I started to realize that there was a story unfolding before my eyes. I began to realize that there was a grand and marvelous story that each individual crystal was trying to tell me.

As soon as I latched onto the idea of publishing my photographs, I talked to several publishers about my idea, but no one seemed interested. Rejection didn't change my determination to have my photographs published, and so I decided that I would publish them on my own. But I soon realized that though I could afford to have the photographs printed and bound into a book, the restrictive distribution system in Japan wouldn't allow me to have the books sold in bookstores.

This seemed like a formidable obstacle, but I just decided not to worry about it. When the completed books arrived, we packed up the books for the few hundred friends and acquaintances who had reserved copies and sent them off. Not long after sending off these first copies, a strange thing started to happen. We started getting reorders from the people who had reserved copies. They had told their friends and acquaintances about the book, and those people had told others. Some people bought five or even ten copies and distributed them to their friends. It indeed seemed like the drop in the pond had become a fast-spreading ripple.

My expectations quickly expanded, and I next wanted people around the world to know what was in this book of photographs, and so I had a translation company translate all the explanations into English. Happily, people from around the world did see the book: Shizuko Ouwehand, a woman who would later serve as my interpreter, sent the book to friends in Europe and America, and this resulted in invitations from people who had seen the photographs to visit those countries and present lectures. Over the years, I have been blessed with opportunities to visit Switzerland, Germany, Australia, the Netherlands, Italy, England, the United States, Canada, and many other countries to introduce the crystals to the people of the world.

Everything seemed to happen at just the right time. People are looking for a way to make sense of this world of chaos that we find ourselves in. This photograph album became a small but meaningful drop that created a ripple, which has since spread throughout the world.

I would like here to introduce only a small portion of the photographs that I have taken. Some of them are included in the work *The Messages of Water*, and some from the second collection of photographs called *The Messages of Water II*, and other photographs were taken especially for this book. You yourself will be able to clearly see the effect that words, photographs, and music can have on water.

These photographs were seen by Japanese as well by people from around the world, many of whom sent me letters with their opinions and thoughts. The pebble that I threw into the pond had indeed created a large ripple that now started to come back to me.

I was astounded to see that so many people were impressed by the effect that the energy of human consciousness and words had on the formation of ice crystals, despite the fact that this idea—that words and thoughts have the power to change water and other substances—may certainly seem like far-out religion or philosophy.

(*Text continues on page 37.*)

We showed words to water

We wrapped a piece of paper with words typed on it around a bottle of water.

Love and gratitude

This crystal is as perfect as can be. This indicates that love and gratitude are fundamental to the phenomenon of life in all of nature.

Thank you (Japanese)

We showed words meaning "thank you" in different languages, always resulting in crystals that were beautiful and complete.

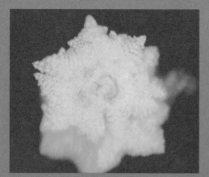

Thank you (English)

Thank you (Chinese)

Danke (German)

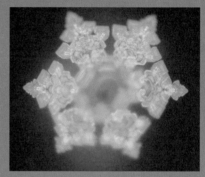

Merci (French)

Thank you (Korean)

Grazie (Italian)

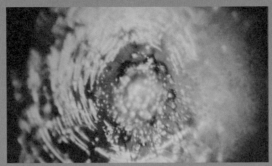

You fool! (Japanese)

You fool! (English)

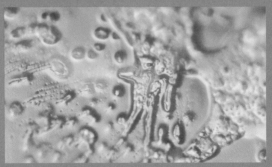

You make me sick. I will kill you. (Japanese)

When words that indicated harm to humans were shown to the water, no crystals formed. It even appears that the words "You make me sick" created the shape of a man with a gun.

Angel (Japanese)

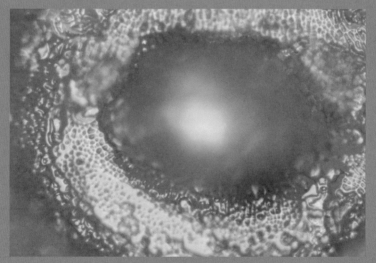

Satan (Japanese)

The word "angel" resulted in a ring of small crystals
linked together, while the word "Satan" formed a crystal
with a dark lump in the center as if ready to attack.

Let's do it! (Japanese)

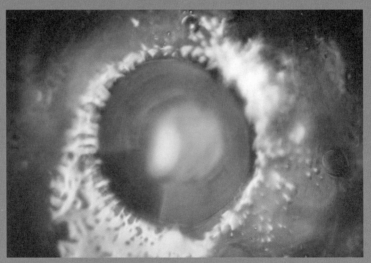

Do it! (Japanese)

"Let's do it!" creates a lovely shape, while "Do it!" creates a crystal similar to that created by the word "Satan." This might indicate that force and commands are alien to the principles of nature.

10

I'm sorry (Japanese)

This shows what a simple "I'm sorry" can result in.
Perhaps the reason the crystal is blurred is because a
simple "I'm sorry" can sound more sincere than a more
elaborate apology.

11

Wisdom (Japanese)

Wisdom (English)

Weisheit (German)

The word "wisdom" in various languages created beautifully formed crystals. This may indicate that wisdom is a basic principle of nature throughout the world.

12

A test conducted at an elementary school

Here are some photographs taken after children at a Japanese elementary school spoke to the water, and also one photograph of water that was ignored.

You're cute

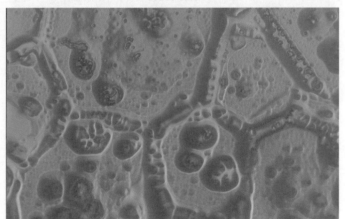
You fool

The children said different things to different bottles of water. When the children said "You're cute" to the water, cute crystals formed, but "You fool" had the opposite effect.

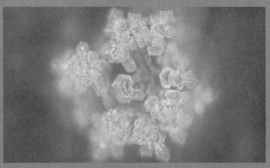

When the children said "You're beautiful" a few times

When the children said "You're beautiful" several times

When the water was ignored

When the water was told "You're beautiful" several times, it resulted in crystals more well-formed than when the water was only told this a few times. The crystal formed by the ignored water was the least complete.

What does the face of the cosmos look like?

Here are photographs of crystals made from water exposed to the word "cosmos" in Japanese, English, and German, and also a crystal formed using a photograph of the earth.

Cosmos (Japanese)

Cosmos (English)

Kosmos (German)

All three crystals are similar, with clearly formed crystals. It appears that the principles of the cosmos transcend language differences.

When shown a photograph of the Earth

The crystal is beautiful, but we can't help but notice that it is a little deformed. If not for this deformity, it would be as beautiful as any complete crystal.

What happens when water is exposed to music?

The following crystal photographs were produced when glass bottles of water were placed between two speakers.

Beethoven: Symphony No. 5

Beethoven: Symphony No. 6 ("Pastoral")

Beethoven's music resulted in fanciful crystals with great detail and exactness, creating a healing effect.

Mozart: Symphony No. 40

This beautiful crystal reflects the beauty of this piece of music. The crystal seems to indicate the unreserved way that Mozart lived his life.

"Air on the G string"

This flowing melody by Bach (in the famous arrangement for violin and piano) is well represented by this crystal.

Chopin: Etude in E major

Chopin: Prelude in D flat major

Piano music seems to create droplet-like crystals.

Tchaikovsky: *Swan Lake*

The top crystal indicates a swan, while the rainbow colors of the bottom crystal seem to represent the light of hope, perhaps affected by the story of Swan Lake.

The Beatles: *Yesterday*

The orthodox form was unexpected. Perhaps this is a result of this song being a favorite throughout the world.

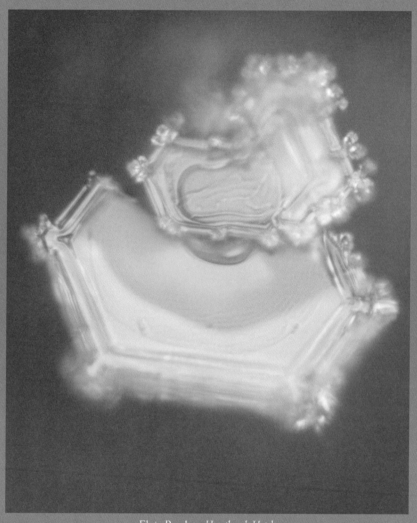

Elvis Presley: *Heartbreak Hotel*

As if to mimic the song, the crystal is divided into two parts.

Bud Powell: *Cleopatra's Dream*

Modern jazz from the 1950s created this beautiful
crystal, indicative of the healing qualities of this music,
created during a period of turmoil.

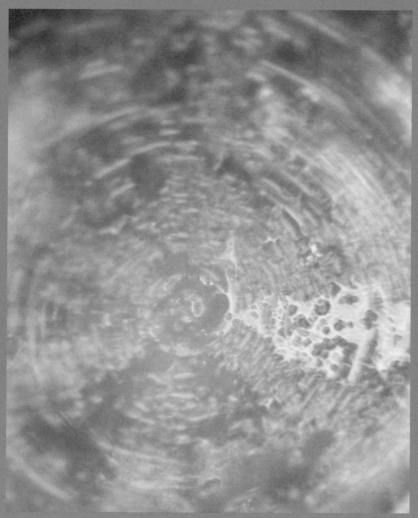

Heavy-metal music

This is the result of loud music full of angry and vulgar lyrics. The result is similar to that created by "You fool!" indicating that water responds more to words than to music.

25

Spring

Autumn

Summer

Winter

Vivaldi: *Four Seasons*

The four seasons are well represented by these crystals: the blossoming of spring, the flowery summer, the promise of new life in mature fall, and the quiet steadiness of winter.

I found a little autumn (from a Japanese nursery song)

Red dragonfly (from a Japanese nursery song)

The words "I found a little autumn" resulted in a small crystal with grains that look like fallen leaves, and the crystal resulting from "Red dragonfly" could be interpreted as six dragonflies with their petal-like wings spread open.

Blooming tangerine trees on a hill

The color of this crystal changed every ten seconds, showing that water also breathes. Perhaps the changing of the center to red indicates the changing color of the tangerine.

Harmful effects of electromagnetic waves

Samples of distilled water and water shown the words "love and gratitude" were placed next to televisions, computers, and mobile telephones, and heated by microwave ovens.

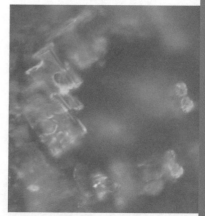

Television

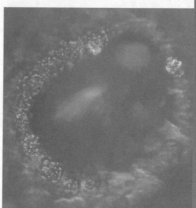

Computer

The water samples shown "love and gratitude" on the left created more complete crystals than the distilled water samples on the right. This would indicate that moderation is needed with televisions and computers.

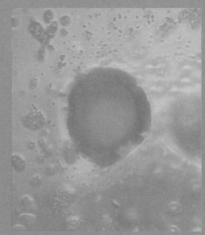

Mobile telephone

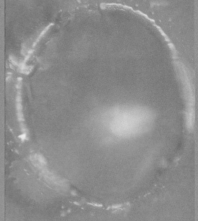

Microwave oven

The distilled water heated in the microwave resulted in a crystal similar to that created by the word "Satan," and the water exposed to the mobile telephone can't be much better for your body.

Water shown a wholesome television show

This beautiful crystal is made from water shown a program about the mysteries of life, showing that the danger of electromagnetic waves changes with the content of the information.

Some unusual crystals

On the following pages are photographs of crystals made from lake water that has been prayed over; water shown the name of Amaterasu, the Shinto sun goddess; and water shown images of crop circles, dolphins, and ground water right before and after an earthquake.

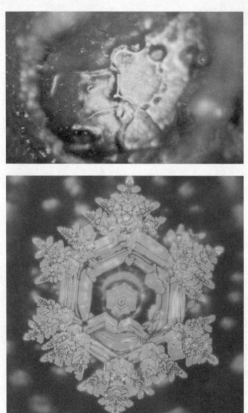

Lake water before and after a Buddhist healing prayer

A priest repeated a healing prayer facing the lake. The first crystal before the prayer looks like a distorted face, but the crystal formed after the prayer looks like a light shining from the galaxy.

Water shown the name of the Amaterasu goddess

This crystal looks like a beautiful mirror or perhaps the outline of the sun. In addition to being beautiful, it radiates with grandeur or even holiness.

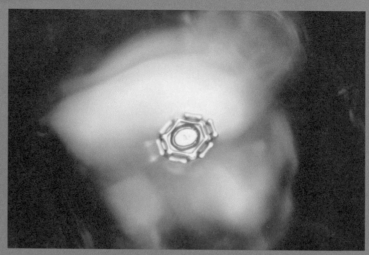

A crystal shown the photograph of a crop circle

Water from a washbasin at the East entrance
of the Heitate Shrine in Kumamoto prefecture

The crystal shown a crop circle looked like a UFO. The
water from Japan's oldest shrine resulted in a crystal that
resembles the shape of the character in Japanese that
means "gratitude."

Water shown a photograph of a dolphin

Dolphins are said to be as intelligent as or more intelligent than human beings, and are said to have healing powers. This noble crystal seems to radiate with healing.

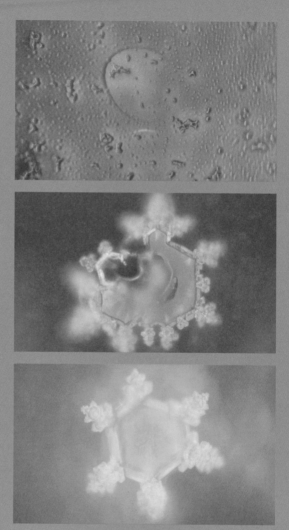

Ground water right before and after an earthquake
in Shimane Prefecture, and later in the same place

Before the earthquake, no crystals were formed, as if the
water were predicting the earthquake. As time passed
after the earthquake, the ability of the water to form
crystals returned.

While some water resulted in crystals of grandeur, as if to symbolize all the beauty of this world, the crystals formed from other water were deformed or nonexistent, as if to tell us something about the dark recesses dormant within the soul.

When I give lectures, I use slides to show my photographs of ice crystals. The reactions to these slides are quite varied. I often hear people gasp in surprise and sometimes even see them shed tears. I have discovered that a single drop of water can have various ripple effects on an individual.

Manuela Kihm, the person who first invited me to give a lecture in Switzerland, expressed her feelings this way when she reacted to the photographs:

> We can see the wonder of the water crystal photographs with our own eyes. As a result, our consciousness makes a rapid leap. This awakening of the consciousness happens almost instantly. The fact that things that we have thought and felt can be seen with our eyes accelerates this change.

Another Swiss participant responded,

> Through the photographs, I could see that the energy of our consciousness and words can

change things that we can actually see with our eyes. This is the first and only way that this elusive energy can be viewed. We don't believe what we can't see, but the ice crystals show us everything—it's no longer about whether you believe or disbelieve. Using this method, anyone can conduct their own experiment and prove it for themselves.

And a Japanese reader wrote,

Water is not just another substance—it is the life force of majestic nature. It made me once again realize the mysterious ability of water to cleanse and give life to all living. I can see that the soul, feelings, and vibration have an effect on the formation of ice crystals, and through this I can feel the importance of the soul and words. This information is extremely wonderful and uniquely impressive.

It appears that ice crystals are closely and permanently linked to the human soul. When I think about why ice crystals have spoken to so many people, I know that it is because they contain the key to the mysteries of the universe, and this key can unlock the consciousness required to understand the proper order of the universe, and our role in it.

Water is the mirror of the soul. It has many faces, formed by aligning itself with the consciousness of human beings. What gives water its ability to reflect what is in people's souls? In order to answer that question, I would first like to make sure that you understand this fact: Existence is vibration.

The entire universe is in a state of vibration, and each thing generates its own frequency, which is unique. All that I have to say in this book is based on this one fact. My years of research into water have taught me that this is the fundamental principle of the universe.

It can be said in just three words, but for people who have never heard them, these are very difficult words to understand.

You might think, *Existence is vibration? Even this table? This chair? My body? How can everything that can be seen and touched be vibration?* It is indeed difficult to believe that things that you can pick up with your hands and examine—things like wood, rocks, and concrete—are all vibrating.

But now the science of quantum mechanics generally acknowledges that substance is nothing more than vibration. When we separate something into its smallest parts, we always enter a strange world where all that exists is particles and waves.

Let's imagine that you could reduce your body to microscopic size, and that you set off on an exploration to discover the secrets of this universe called *you*. You would soon see that each thing consists of nothing more than atoms, each atom being a nucleus with electrons rotating around it. The number and shape of these electrons and their orbits give each substance a particular set of vibrational frequencies. You would discover that whatever the substance, nothing is solid. Instead there is only a nucleus surrounded by an endlessly rotating wave.

Everything is eternally moving and vibrating—on and off, at an incredible speed.

According to the *Hanyashingyo*, the Buddhist *Wisdom and Heart Sutra*, "That which can be seen has no form, and that which cannot be seen has form." We can now say that this strange contradiction, spoken ages ago by the Buddha, has been proved true by modern science.

Our eyes can see objects, but they can't see vibration. However, I'd like you to ask yourself if you haven't had an experience similar to the following:

You are talking with someone in a room, and the mood is warm, friendly, and free-flowing. Then another person enters the room. The moment they open the door, you notice a change in the atmosphere, and now instead of warmth filling the room, the space is encased in a dark and cold mood.

You look at the new arrival's face and see a haggard expression and humped-over shoulders, someone who looks like they are just tired with life. What could be the cause of this pain? Maybe a broken heart, a mistake at work, or just general disgust with life—I'll leave it up to you. What I want you to think about is why the mood in the room changed the moment that the door was opened.

Human beings are also vibrating, and each individual vibrates at a unique frequency. Each one of us has the sensory skills necessary to feel the vibrations of others.

A person experiencing great sadness will emit a sadness frequency, and someone who is always joyful and living life fully will emit a corresponding frequency. A person who loves others will send out a frequency of love, but from a person who acts out evil will come a dark and evil frequency.

This same principle also applies to objects and locations. For example, there are locations where accidents frequently happen, locations where businesses succeed, and locations that create happiness. And you might have heard about a jewel that brings tragedy to successive owners.

This applies not only to physical objects, but the various phenomena that go on in the world also emit characteristic frequencies. A change in the energy of the atmosphere results in lightning and storms. Intense energy will result in natural disasters, but we need to realize that these are not evil events. If we consider the enormous amount of evil energy being blown away, perhaps we should actually be appreciative of lightning and storms.

For another illustration, think about the fact that people around the world enjoy coming together to celebrate. When people gather, wear special clothes, sing and dance, and are festive, the result is that stagnant and evil vibrations are dissipated and joyous vibrations are created.

All things vibrate, and they vibrate at their own frequencies. When you understand this, you will significantly broaden your understanding of the universe. With this understanding, your eyes will open to things you have never seen before—things previously pushed to the back of your consciousness—and these discoveries and feelings will give new life to your soul.

The fact that everything is in a state of vibration also means that everything is creating sound.

This doesn't mean that we can hear every sound, although there are some people who apparently hear the voices of trees and who can communicate with plants. Whether we can hear the sound or not, we can say that the unique frequency of all objects can be interpreted as sound.

It is said that the human ear is generally capable of hearing frequencies from approximately 15 Hz to

20,000 Hz (Hz, or Hertz, indicates the number of cycles of the repetitive waveform per second). Actually, it's a good thing that our ears have such limits—otherwise we probably wouldn't be able to sleep at night.

The natural world is indeed well designed—everything is in balance. And as sound is created, there is a *master listener* to receive the sound: water.

Let me ask you to think about why crystal formation would be affected by music, and why completely different results would be reached depending on the spoken and written words water was exposed to. The answer is found, again, in the fact that everything is vibration. Water—so sensitive to the unique frequencies being emitted by the world—essentially and efficiently mirrors the outside world.

Music and spoken words are vibration, they are easily understood and interpreted by just about anyone. Sounds like the chant created by a human voice at a Buddhist funeral create a healing frequency.

But how can we interpret the phenomena of crystal formation being affected by words written on paper and shown to water? The written words themselves actually emit a unique vibration that the water is capable of sensing. Water faithfully mirrors all the vibrations created in the world, and changes these vibrations into a form that can be seen with the human eye. When water is shown a written word, it receives it as vibration, and expresses the message in a specific form. (You might think of letters as being a visual code for expressing words.)

But what, fundamentally, are words? The Old Testament states, "In the beginning there was the Word." This would mean that before the creation of the universe, there existed "the Word." My interpretation of this is that "the Word" created human beings, and human beings then learned *words* from nature.

In primeval times, when people lived within nature, they needed to protect themselves, and so they were sensitive to the frequencies and sounds generated by nature, in order to detect danger before it could sneak up on them.

The sound of the wind blowing, the sound of water flowing, the sound of an animal walking through the grass—the ability to understand these sounds and relay them to others using one's voice was required for survival. It is likely that these attempts at language were simple messages of a few words, but with the development of culture and accumulation of experience, our vocabulary expanded.

Why, then, are the languages that people speak so diverse? This is quite easy to understand if you consider that language is learned from the vibrations of the natural environment. The natural environment varies greatly with location, and each environment will create different vibrations. The volatile weather climate of Europe and the humid islands of Asia all create different vibrations that flow out of nature. In Japan, there are four distinct seasons, and so the Japanese language reflects this with a beautiful lexicon of weather-related words.

Water exposed to the words "Thank you" formed beautiful geometric crystals, no matter what the language. But water exposed to "You fool" and other degrading words resulted in obviously broken and deformed crystals.

According to the Bible, before the Tower of Babel all people spoke the same language. Perhaps this is telling us that even though location and natural environment differ, the fundamental principles of nature are the same.

We can surmise that when a complete geometric crystal is formed, water is in alignment with nature and the phenomenon we call life. The crystals do not form in water that has been polluted by the results of our failure to remember the laws of nature. When we tried taking photographs of crystals from Tokyo's tap water, the results were pitiful. This is because the water is sanitized with chlorine, thus damaging the innate ability of water to form crystals.

When water freezes, the particles of water link together to form the crystal nucleus, and when the nucleus grows in a stable way into a hexagonal shape, a visible water crystal appears; but when information in conflict with nature is present, an incomplete crystal will be formed.

The words *gratitude* and *love* form the fundamental principles of the laws of nature and the phenomenon of life. Therefore, water in its natural form is required to create the hexagonal form. By contrast, words such as "You fool" do not exist in nature and are instead unnatural elements created by people. Words that revile, harm, and ridicule are the result of the culture created by humans.

It's likely that only vibrations of love and gratitude appear in nature, and observation of nature shows this to be true. The trees and plants show respect for each other by the way they live in harmony. This also applies to the animal kingdom. Even lions only kill when hungry, and never at random. The plants in the shadows of the trees do not complain, and the animals do not try to take more food than they require.

In an article in the March–April 1989 issue of the American scientific journal *21st Century Science and Technology*, Warren J. Hamerman wrote that the organic matter that forms human beings generates a frequency that can be represented by sound at approximately forty-two octaves above middle C (the note near the center of the piano keyboard). The modern standard for middle C is approximately 262 Hz, so this means that the sound reaches roughly 570 trillion Hz. Since Hz means vibrations per second, this indicates that human beings vibrate 570 trillion times a second, a number that exceeds the imagination and indicates incredible and wonderful hidden potential.

It is difficult to conceive forty-two octaves, but just realize that the frequency of the human being is immensely diverse and unparalleled. The human being holds a universe within, filled with overlapping frequencies, and the result is a symphony of cosmic proportions.

When I talk to people about vibration and frequency, I use what I like to call the *"Do-re-mi-fa-so-la-ti* theory." This simple theory just means that the frequency of everything in the cosmos can be summarized in seven parts—*do, re, mi, fa, so, la,* and *ti.*

The universe consists of an uncountable number of things ranging from the lowest to the highest frequency. It might help to imagine keys aligned in order on a piano keyboard, starting from the lowest sound. If you press down on the white keys, you will hit *do, re, mi, fa, so, la,* and *ti* When you move up the keyboard one octave, from one *do* to the next, the frequency doubles. In other words, the doubling of frequencies divided into seven parts is *do, re, mi, fa, so, la,* and *ti.* Therefore, the repeating of these seven sounds expresses all sound from the lowest to the highest.

But what enlightenment can be obtained by seeing frequency as sound?

The most important revelation is that of resonance. Sounds of the same frequency resonate. This can be understood by making use of a tuning fork, a Y-shaped instrument used to tune the pitch of an instrument or voice.

When a tuning fork is hit with a rubber hammer, creating a *la* sound, and a singer responds with a *la*, the tuning fork and the voice create a single frequency sound wave. This is called resonance. When one side creates a frequency and the other responds with the same sound, they resonate. It's said that likes attract, and so it would appear that vibrations attract and interact with each other.

With some careful observation, you'll see that this same phenomenon is going on all around you. A dog walking along the street may not respond to other animals it passes but will be very responsive to a dog on the other side of the street. Dogs will often howl when they hear the sound of a siren, and this could also be a type of resonance.

And we see this in human relationships: people who generate similar frequencies are attracted to each other, resulting in friendship. Certain people remain uninterested in each other, no matter how physically close they may be. However, if someone you don't like approaches you and you react, this also means that you are resonating in some way with that person.

The greatest secret of Japanese martial arts is referred to as "winning without fighting." This essentially means avoiding resonating with the enemy. To fight and win results in resonance with the enemy, and so the level of the relationship is very low.

When frequencies are fundamentally incompatible, they cannot resonate. We cannot accept what is fundamentally different from us.

However, an interesting fact is that resonance can result even when frequencies are not identical. This happens, for instance, when the frequency is doubled. Playing the *la* key on the piano at 440 Hz and the *la* key an octave lower at 220 Hz creates quite a pleasant resonating sound, and responding to a tuning fork with a sound one octave lower also creates nice resonance.

When the frequency difference is twofold, fourfold, eightfold, and so on—or one-half, one-quarter, and so on—the result is resonance. The principle of this relationship extends to infinity. No matter how distant the frequencies, resonance will result if one of the two numbers is a multiple of the other. We can also say that for every sound on each level there is a resonating sound on every other level.

When you think about it, people are attracted to Christ, Buddha, and others who emit a high level of vibration, but we also find ourselves attracted to the low-level outlaws of society (such as Bonnie and Clyde). This may seem like an inconsistency, but it can be explained by the fact that people resonate with others on various levels. Perhaps this dichotomy is a natural part of life.

It might help our understanding in this area to consider how to interpret, from a vibration-frequency perspective, the phenomenon of two people falling in love.

Love is one type of resonance. If, for example, you have a frequency-level capability of 10, you will resonate with others on that same level, or perhaps with someone on a level a little higher, say 12.

When people resonate and fall in love, they rise to their highest level of capability. If a person with a capability of 10 who has only been using 5 parts of that capacity falls in love with someone with a level of 12, then he or she will naturally make use of the level-10 capability and show an increase in frequency.

When you are in love, you perform better at work, and the work that you do (and often your environment) may well change without you realizing it. People who continue to do superior work well into old age are almost inevitably in love. Of course, this love is not limited to romantic love. It also can include a loving respect and attraction towards other people. Love has the effect of raising our frequency level and making us shine. Wouldn't it be wonderful if we could be in love for a lifetime?

Most of the objects found in nature emit stable frequencies. Each sparrow sounds basically the same (though the sparrows themselves might recognize slight differences), and the sounds made by dogs or cats do not have a great deal of variation. By contrast, the human being is able to make full use of the *do, re, mi, fa, so, la, ti* scale to create beautiful melodies. Wouldn't you agree that this is indeed a marvelous ability?

Humans are the only creatures that have the capacity to resonate with all other creatures and objects found in nature. We can speak with all that exists in the universe. We can give out energy and also receive energy in return. However, this is ability is a two-edged sword. When people act out only on their own greed, they emit an energy that serves to destroy the harmony within nature.

The defiling of our earth is the result of an unrelenting hunger for convenience and the fulfillment of greed, initiated by the industrial revolution. This has led to lifestyles of mass consumption that seriously threaten the global environment.

We have embarked on a new century, a time in history when we must make serious changes in the way that we think. Only the human can resonate with the rest of the world, and this is why it is so essential that we change our thinking, so we can live in harmony with nature and not go on destroying the earth. What vibration we give to the earth and what kind of planet we create depends on each one of us as individuals.

How will you choose to live your life?

If you fill your heart with love and gratitude, you will find yourself surrounded by so much that you can love and that you can feel grateful for, and you can even get closer to enjoying the life of health and happiness that you seek. But what will happen if you emit signals of hate, dissatisfaction, and sadness? Then you will probably find yourself in a situation that makes you hateful, dissatisfied, and sad.

The life you live and the world you live in are up to you.

The Portal into a Different World

Now I'd like to ask you to put down this book, pour a glass of water, and place it on the table before you. (Or, if that's not possible, imagine that you have done it.)

What do you see in the glass?

You can see the room that you're in, the scenery from the window, and the overall feeling around you— all recorded by the water.

Water is something so common that we seldom pause to think about it. Although we drink it, wash with it, and cook with it every day of our lives, few people spend much time seriously thinking about water. But there is probably nothing more mysterious.

One of the most mysterious things about water is the simple fact that ice floats in it. When other substances move from the liquid to the solid state, the density of the molecules and atoms that form the solid increases, and the substance becomes relatively heavier. However, water particles align in a very regulated way, with many large spaces between them. When ice returns to water, the particles become hundreds of thousands of times more active. As the particles become more active, the spaces fill in, making the liquid form of water denser and heavier than the solid form.

Water is at its heaviest at 4°C (39°F). This is the temperature at which the active water particles fill the empty spaces of the molecular structure. As the temperature increases, the particles become even more active, which then lowers the density.

For this reason, no matter how cold the temperature is above a lake (or other such body of water), the temperature at the bottom remains stable at 4°C. The result is that the living creatures of the lake are able to survive long winters under the ice.

If water behaved like other substances, and ice sank to the bottom, then what would happen? For one thing, we would probably not be here. Every time the temperature dropped, the bottoms of the lakes and oceans would become solid ice, and all living creatures would die.

Due to the fact that ice floats, even when the surface of water becomes covered in ice, the environment below the ice allows life to go on.

Water also has the unique ability to dissolve other substances and carry them away. Think about how much matter can be dissolved into water, and how difficult it is to return water to its original pure state. At semiconductor plants and chemical factories, special water purifiers are used to secure water that is extremely pure, but as soon as this water is placed in a container made of plastic (or most other substances), impurities begin to dissolve. Maintaining water in a completely pure state is extremely difficult. It will not surprise you to learn that even tap water and water from streams that look perfectly clear contains many impurities and minerals.

This ability of water to dissolve other substances creates a type of "soup of life" that supplies the oceans with the necessary nutrients that enable life. This *soup* became the birthplace of all living creatures on the earth.

Indeed, water is the force that creates and gives life. Without water, particles wouldn't mix together or circulate. Water created chaos on the earth and it also gave birth to order—resulting in a planet overflowing with life.

It is an ancient belief that where there is water there is life. In Japan, a place where water rose up from the ground was considered to be sacred and to have high energy levels, making it the ideal spot for erecting a shrine. Other spots were also designated as sacred because of the "path of energy" they emitted, and such spots were almost inevitably found to be above underground water.

Water is the mother of life, while also being the energy for life. This is possible because of the unique characteristics of water.

My investigation into the mysteries of water makes me think that water is something not of this earth.

Why do you think there is so much water on the earth? Most explanations say that when the earth was formed some 4.6 billion years ago, water turned to steam, evaporated, and formed rain that fell on the earth, resulting in the creation of the oceans.

But it all started with the birth of the sun. Lumps of gas came together and started rotating, forming a red ball. The remaining dust and gasses came together and formed the earth and the other planets in the solar system. At this time, the earth was still a ball of burning magma that contained hydrogen. As the magma cooled, the hydrogen evaporated into the newly formed atmosphere.

But not all scholars agree with this theory, and some offer radically different alternatives. One such scholar is Louis Frank of the University of Iowa, who has proposed that water arrived on this planet in the form of lumps of ice from outer space.

Professor Frank began his investigation when he became puzzled by the fact that satellite photographs showed black spots; he reached the conclusion that these black spots were small comets that were falling to earth.

These mini-comets are actually balls of water and ice weighing a hundred tons or more, and falling into the earth's atmosphere at a rate of about twenty per minute (or ten million per year). The theory is that these balls of ice bombarded the earth forty billion years ago, creating the seas and oceans, and this same phenomenon continues today.

As the earth's gravity pulls these ice comets into the atmosphere, the heat of the sun evaporates them and turns them into gas. As they fall fifty-five kilometers from outer space, the gas particles mix with the air in the atmosphere and are blown about, falling to the earth as rain or snow.

A few years ago, an announcement by NASA and the University of Hawaii that Dr. Frank's theory does have credibility was widely publicized by the media, but there are still many scientists who refuse to accept this new way of looking at the world.

If this new approach were to gain widespread credibility, it would require many of the books in the world's libraries to be rewritten. It would have an impact on almost all of the scientific theories related to life on this planet, such as the origin of man and Darwin's theory of evolution.

It is universally accepted that there can be no life without water, and if we accept that water, the source of all life, was sent from outer space, then logic leads us to the conclusion that all life, include that of human beings, is alien to this planet.

But if we go along with this theory of water being extraterrestrial, then perhaps we can better understand the many unusual characteristics of water.

Why does ice float? Why is water able to dissolve so much? Why is a towel able to soak up water, seemingly in defiance of the laws of gravity? From the standpoint that water is not of this world, these and other mysteries surrounding water may seem a little less difficult to understand.

Water from outer space—it might seem a little too farfetched. But doesn't it also tickle your imagination? After water has completed its long journey through the cosmos, it begins its next phase of travels on our planet.

The lumps of ice arrive on earth, and then they become clouds and eventually fall to the earth as rain or snow. The water then washes the mountains, seeps into the ground becoming rich in minerals, and then rises to the surface again. From rivers to oceans, the sun evaporates water and returns it to the atmosphere to once again form clouds.

This water, and the minerals that it carries through this cycle, are what make life possible. The carbon dioxide in the atmosphere melts into the oceans and enables photosynthesis, creating a perfectly balanced ecological system.

The ocean is where the first speck of life emerged, some 3.8 billion years ago. The speck evolved into algae capable of photosynthesis, resulting in the first supply of oxygen. This oxygen, interacting with ultraviolet rays from the sun, encased the earth in a protective vale called the ozone layer.

Then, some 420 million years ago, life took its first step out of the water, and freed itself from the depths of the ocean with the help of oxygen and the ozone layer.

The birth of our humanoid parents is believed to have taken place only 20 million years ago in Africa. If we consider the earth's 4.6 billion year history as constituting one "year," the human being was born at eight o'clock in the evening on the final day—all made possible by the formation of oxygen and the ozone layer.

And the force that created life and allowed life to evolve was, of course, water. Water was able to do this because it has the unique ability to dissolve the required nutrients for life and carry them from the mountains and rivers into the oceans.

So next we ask ourselves if this grand drama of life is just an accident. When we think of the plot that began at a time so distant in the past as to tax our imaginations—the birth of life on this planet, leading to the creation of a perfect system that enabled evolution—we cannot help but feel that a grand intention was somehow involved.

Kazuo Murakami, professor emeritus of Tsukuba University, received global attention for interpreting the oxide DNA code called *renin*. His take on this question is that the more you understand DNA, the more you are forced to admit that some hand played a role in the recording of so much minute and elaborate information in such small spaces. The term he uses to describe this existence is *something great*.

The grand drama of water and life cannot be explained if we exclude the existence of *something great*. Even now the storyboard continues to unfold, in accordance with the scenario written by the grand intentions of the cosmos.

What information did ancient water bring with it when it left outer space and fell to earth? We can assume that it carried the program needed for the development of life. And now I hope you are beginning to get a clearer image of what life is all about.

Water that falls from the sky takes scores or sometimes hundreds of years to seep into the ground and become groundwater. Joan S. Davis of the Zurich Technical University has conducted research into river water for some thirty years in Switzerland, and she refers to it with the expression *wise water*. By contrast, she refers to water that has recently fallen as *juvenile water*.

In the process of falling to the earth, seeping into the ground, and then emerging, water obtains information from various minerals and becomes *wise*.

After thirty years as a professor, Joan has retired from the university, and now conducts her own research. At a symposium in Switzerland, I had the honor of giving a presentation alongside her. The focus of her research is water processing. The current system of supplying water through long pipes results in water that is not extremely healthy for the body. When water is exposed to high pressure and flows straight through pipes, the water clusters break down, letting minerals escape.

And so Joan has focused her attention on finding simple ways to supply healthy water to large numbers of people, including the poor. One of her suggestions is to use crystals: when small ice crystals are introduced into water, the minerals in the water are retained, resulting in water that grows healthier crops. She has also conducted research into improving the quality of water using magnets, and designing water taps to give circular movement to the water. She wants to know how natural movement can be introduced into the way water is supplied.

Joan has the following to say about her research:

I have heard from many people with interest in your research into ice crystals. I think that this research will give people some important suggestions. One suggestion is to give more respect to water. Another is to become aware that water responds to even delicate energy. I also want to let scientists and officials know that there is almost no protection currently being provided for water.

I feel that my research can be used in the fields of health and medical care. There is not much interest in the importance of the physical characteristics of water. For example, it is said that mineral water is good for you, but there are few people who know that the minerals of mineral water can cause hardening of the arteries. Also, mineral water that is carbonated has a high acidity, making it unhealthy for the body. In any case, we need to avoid water that comes in a bottle and replace it with naturally flowing water. Water wants to be free.

Joan also relayed the following:

> The important thing is that we recover our desire to treat water with respect. In our modern culture, we have lost our attitude of respect for water. In ancient Greece, people paid true respect to water, and many Greek myths are based on the protection of water. But then science appeared, and rejected these myths because they were not scientific. Water lost its mystique and became just another substance that technology could clean up as necessary. We sometimes say, "Purified water is not pure." Water processed in treatment plants is not the water that forms beautiful crystals. What water requires is not purification but respect.

These wise words are the result of many years spent observing water. It was extremely encouraging to have such an accomplished scientist express interest in my research into crystals, out of respect for water.

And finally, Joan gave me the following advice:

> If you are able to establish the physical foundations for your theories concerning ice crystals, you will be able to make an announcement to the world as very convincing research here,

since Switzerland is highly recognized throughout the world for its research into water.

This was indeed encouraging for me at a time when
I was planning to establish a center in Switzerland to
promote my research into water.

Water records information, and then while circulating throughout the earth distributes information. This
water sent from the universe is full of the information of
life, and one way to decipher this information is
through the observation of ice crystals.

When I see the many beautiful crystals formed
from water, I get the feeling that I'm looking at the
materialization of life before my eyes. The crystals that
are formed when water is shown positive words are
simply beautiful. The response of water to *love* and *gratitude* is nothing less than grandeur. These positive words
give spirit to water, which materializes it, to reveal life
at its fullest.

I also have the impression that the act of looking at
water crystals is an act of creating life. This is because
when we look at the crystals, the water changes its
appearance moment by moment. Your gaze has a special
energy of its own, and while a gaze of good intentions
will give courage, an evil gaze will actual take it away.

A family that subscribed to our magazine conducted an interesting experiment. They put rice in two

glass jars, and every day for a month said "Thank you" to one jar and "You fool" to the other, and then they tracked how the rice changed over the period. Even the children, when they got home from school, would speak these words to the jars of rice.

After a month, the rice that was told "Thank you" started to ferment, with a mellow smell like that of malt, while the rice that was exposed to "You fool" rotted and turned black.

I wrote about this experiment in the book that I published, and as a result hundreds of families throughout Japan conducted this same experiment for themselves. Everyone reported the same results. One family tried a variation of the experiment: like the others, they said "Thank you" to the first bottle of rice and "You fool" to the second bottle, and then they prepared a third bottle of rice that they simply ignored.

What do you think happened? The rice that was ignored actually rotted before the rice that was exposed to "You fool." When others tried this same experiment, the results were again the same. It seems that being ridiculed is actually not as damaging as being ignored.

To give your positive or negative attention to something is a way of giving energy. The most damaging form of behavior is withholding your attention.

I think that this experiment has the potential to teach us a very important lesson. We must take care to give our children our attention, and to talk with them. Speaking words of kindness and love should begin from the time of conception.

Treating your houseplants gently—looking on them kindly, and speaking words of praise—will help to make them healthy and alive. This also applies to pets and even insects.

Through this book, I hope that many more people will gain respect for water and look at water in a kinder way. The result will be that water will produce more beautiful crystals, and in this way we will be participating in the creation of a small but beautiful world.

I have no doubt that God greatly enjoys his work and wants to give us the same ability that he has—the ability of creation. Then he will look down upon us with gentle eyes, as we use our free agency to choose how we will use this ability.

The memory of life arrived on this earth carried by the soul of water. From this memory, life awoke, the human being emerged, and finally you and I were born. And now once again we look at water and breathe life into it. Your consciousness, awareness, and good will, and your smile from a feeling of love, all give new life to water and result in the creation of a new and glorious universe.

CHAPTER THREE

Consciousness Creates All

Since becoming entranced by the wondrous powers of water, I have been blessed with the opportunity to see and conduct experiments on many types of water from around the world. Each sample of water from a different part of the world has its own unique and beautiful characteristics.

I have also seen with my own eyes how the water of the world is becoming polluted. The World Trade Organization has stated that the twentieth century started with wars for oil, but that in the twenty-first century we will see wars for water.

I mentioned that there is no tap water in Japan that is capable of forming complete and whole crystals, due to the use of chlorine. Chlorine, introduced at the beginning of the twentieth century in London, has been used in Japan for more than fifty years now.

In contrast to tap water, the water from springs, the upper reaches of rivers, and other such natural sources creates beautiful crystals. However, most of the water that is now emerging from the ground fell from the clouds more than fifty years ago—about the time that industrialization began in Japan.

Pollution of rainwater has reached a global scale. I tried to take photographs of crystals formed using tap water from a city in Japan which had been polluted with dioxin, but I couldn't get the water to produce even a shadow of a crystal. Industrial waste circulates, polluting water as it goes, and spreading toxins throughout the world.

But there is hope. The people of the city with the dioxin-polluted water have became very interested in protecting their water, and now each year it is becoming easier and easier to form crystals.

Pollution originated within our own consciousness. We started to think that we wanted a bountiful and convenient lifestyle at any cost, and this selfishness led to the pollution of the environment that now affects every corner of the globe.

We have seen through the crystal photographs that water is the mirror of our souls. What do our souls look like—and how should they look? These are questions that can also be answered by water.

In what direction are we headed? What is our role in protecting this planet? Such questions can only be considered when we recognize the greatness of the human being. Perhaps it is time that we stop seeing the human being as the evil agent. I think we underestimate the innate abilities that we each have. We have enormous power.

Scientists estimate that there are between 108 and 111 elements. (I suspect that the number is 108—for reasons which I'll explain.) Thus far, 90 elements have been verified in the human body—of all the creatures alive, only the human body contains so many elements. But I suspect that there are still elements left to be discovered within us (or that we will obtain the remaining elements as we evolve, moving closer to becoming complete human beings).

The more evolved creatures contain a greater array of elements. Compared with human beings, plants contain far fewer elements, and what is the result of having fewer elements? We can deduce that fewer elements means a smaller capacity for emotions. Other animals can feel pain, but it's most likely that only humans (and other animals close in evolution to humans) are capable of the higher emotions of sadness and passion.

If we consider that the human body is a universe within itself, it is only natural to conclude that we carry within us all the elements. According to Buddhism, the human being is born with 108 earthly desires (such as confusion, attachment, jealousy, and vanity), which torture us throughout our lives. I think it is logical to conclude that these 108 earthly desires have counterparts in the 108 elements.

In fact, the first vibration-detection device that I introduced to Japan went a long way toward proving this. The device was capable of measuring the unique vibrations emitted around us and then transcribing them into water. I was able to measure the vibrations coming from many different people, and I realized that the negative vibrations that we emit correspond to the vibrations emitted by the various elements.

For example, the vibrations created by irritation are equivalent to those of mercury, by anger to those of lead, and by sadness and sorrow to those of aluminum. In the same way, uncertainty is related to cadmium, despair to steel, and stress to zinc.

In recent years, it has been pointed out that the use of aluminum pans and cooking utensils may be a contributing factor in Alzheimer's disease. If this is true, then it is likely that it is because aluminum has the same vibrational frequency as sadness, and so the sadness and sorrow of old age calls out to aluminum, leading to the onset of Alzheimer's.

Joan Davis, the water scientist in the previous chapter, related the following interesting episode:

A physicist conducted an experiment in which he studied how the positions of the stars affected water. Using water containing various minerals, he tested how easily paper soaked up the water when the stars were in certain positions.

What he found was that when Saturn has a large influence on Earth, lead responded by being soaked up by the paper, while other elements such as copper, silver, and steel showed little or no response.

We can deduce from this that there is a close connection between Saturn and lead. Metals resonate the emotions and moods of people, and so the next logical deduction is that Saturn is closely related to the emotion of anger.

Perhaps the relationship between the constellations and personality talked about by astrologers and others may have something to do with the relationship with metals.

This is a very meaningful theory for me, especially since I have my own ideas about the relationship between the 108 earthly desires and the elements. The number of planets in the solar system is 9, a number that when multiplied by 12 gives us 108. Using the periodic table, we may someday be able to identify which planets correlate to which elements.

Even as I wrote the draft for this book, I saw a television program that said all the elements on earth were created by the high heat of a star exploding in distant outer space. Just one more interesting piece of the puzzle.

Throughout our lives, we will be subject to the 108 earthly desires, but how should we deal with these negative emotions that seem so impossible to avoid? Knowing how to deal with these negative feelings is the same knowledge that we need to get along well in this life. So what should we do if we find our minds full of anger, sadness, envy, or other negative thoughts?

We first need to understand that is not possible or necessary to rid ourselves of our emotions. There isn't anyone who is completely free from negative thoughts. We all carry within us a memory of our ancestors from the distant past, beginning with the awakening of the first human being, and we are all destined to inherit a portion of their negativity.

However, it is indeed painful to be unable to free ourselves from constant negative thoughts and feelings that eat away at our souls. If only for a moment, how can we go about freeing ourselves from all of the negativity?

Based on the principles of vibration, the answer is very clear. All we need to do is emit the emotion that is opposite to the negative emotion. By combining two opposite waves, the negative emotion disappears.

A few years back, a university in Japan developed a method for erasing sound with sound. They would create one noise that would serve to erase the unwanted noise, and thus create a quiet space (for example, around a telephone). By identifying the wavelength of the unwanted noise, the researchers were able to create the exact opposite noise and broadcast it from speakers, completely wiping out the sound in a specific area. This same method has already been used to negate the noise made by automobile engines.

There are parallels to this principle for human emotions. For every negative emotion, there is an exactly opposite positive emotion. The following list contains emotions that create opposing frequencies:

hate	gratitude
anger	kindness
fear	courage
anxiety	peace of mind
pressure	presence of mind

The fact that two opposite emotions issue the same wave is significant for two reasons. First, like Jekyll and Hyde, we all have two faces. You probably are aware that people with short tempers tend to be quick to cry, and that it's not uncommon for someone who everyone sees as being a good person to suddenly commit a crime. We frequently hear about a man who is kind and gentle to his girlfriend, but who becomes threatening and violent as soon as she talks about leaving him.

While there is no one who hasn't an evil bone in their body, there is also no one who is totally evil to the core. The fact that someone harbors opposing emotions simply makes them human.

If you have been made sick by the emotion of hate, then you need to look for healing in the emotion of appreciation.

But even if you know this, it still may be difficult to fill your heart with gratitude if it is already filled with hate for others. At such times, it might be helpful to rely on the services of a healer. Perhaps it is possible that the miracle water of Lourdes in France, which is said to have healing powers, is filled with the feelings of appreciation of the Mother Mary. As a result, people who have been made ill by the vibrations of hate can be miraculously healed by drinking this holy water.

This is the same principle involved in homeopathy. Why, when a poison is diluted in water to the point where it can no longer be physically detected, does the previously toxic solution then becomes therapeutic? When the substance itself is gone, and all that is left is the information from the vibration, both poison and medicine become the same.

Logically thinking, medicine is not good for the body. It may alleviate symptoms and get rid of pain, but medicine can also become a powerful poison.

Medicine that gets rid of pain happens to have the opposite vibrational frequency of the targeted pain. By mixing various substances together in a lab, you'll be able to find the frequency that you are looking for. When you inject the substance into a mouse and get the desired effect, you can then try giving the substance to humans.

When the medicine enters the body and stops the pain, the vibrations from the combined substances stop, and the various substances return to their original states, in which they emit their original vibrations. However, if these vibrations happen to damage other cell structures, then harmful side effects will result.

Medicine is useful in the treatment of illness, but we don't really understand why medicine works. When you look at medicine from the standpoint of vibration, you get a totally different picture. For example, during an operation the damaged vibrational frequency is treated with a much more powerful frequency. Let's say that you fall from a building and hit the ground. At the moment of impact, your body's frequency increases many hundreds of times, creating an obviously critical situation. Dramatic and sudden changes in the body's frequency result in great pain and damage. In such cases, treatment must involve equal or stronger frequencies to be effective—often having to do with the scalpel. Sharp instruments, by nature, have a high frequency, and it's the surgeon's job to use such instruments to cut into the body and return the patient's frequency to normal.

In my opinion, a doctor who treats the human body must first be a philosopher. In the past, the doctor was the community shaman or priest, exhorting people to follow the laws of nature, live their lives correctly, and make use of the healing powers found in nature.

If doctors were to treat not only the sick parts of the body but also the human consciousness, then I think we would see a great reduction in the need for doctors and hospitals. People with ailments would go to their nearby philosopher, for help in understanding the mistakes they have made, and then go home determined to live a better life. It may well be that the physicians of the future will be more like counselors than the doctors we have today.

I have talked with many people about their health problems, and I have come to see that ailments are largely a result of negative emotions. If you can erase the cause of such emotions, you have an innate capacity to recover from illness. The importance of being positive cannot be underestimated.

Positive thinking will strengthen your immune system and help to set you moving towards recovery—a fact that the medical community is starting to wake up to. For instance, there is a doctor who treats his cancer patients with mountain climbing. Giving people a reason to live boosts their spirits and their immune systems.

There is also an increase in interest in holistic medicine—not only treating the symptoms of the illness, but overseeing the patient's lifestyle and psychological well-being. In fact, doctors have recently formed an organization, called the Japan Holistic Medical Society, to promote this type of medicine in Japan.

The days of believing only that which can be seen by the naked eye have passed, and we are now starting to open our eyes to the importance of the soul. It's a move in the right direction, and I think it will become the way the majority thinks within this century.

The human body is essentially water, and consciousness is the soul. Methods that help water to flow smoothly are superior to all other medical methods available to us. It's all about keeping the soul in an unpolluted state. Can you imagine what it would be like to have water capable of forming beautiful crystals flowing throughout your entire body? It can happen if you let it.

Among all medicines, there are none with the healing powers of love. Since I came to this realization, I have continued to tell people that *immunity is love*. What could be more effective at overcome negative powers and returning vitality to the body?

However, I have recently felt the need to change my terminology. I now know that it is not love alone that forms immunity, but love and gratitude. I became convinced of this from the following experiment.

I heated water in a microwave oven and then attempted to see the impact of the magnetic field on crystals. I used two types of water: distilled water, and water from the tap shown the words *love* and *gratitude*. The crystals formed from the distilled water were deformed and incomplete, but the water shown the words *love* and *gratitude* formed complete crystals. In other words, *love* and *gratitude* were able to make the water immune to the damaging effects of the magnetic field.

I have mentioned that water shown the words *love* and *gratitude* forms the most beautiful crystals. Of course the word *love* alone has the ability to create wonderful crystals, but *love* and *gratitude* combine to give the crystals a unique depth and refinement, a diamond-like brilliance.

I also discovered that the *love* and *gratitude* crystals actually look more like the *gratitude* crystals than the *love* crystals. What this indicates is that the *gratitude* vibration is more powerful and has a greater influence. Love tends to be a more active energy, the act of giving oneself unconditionally. By contrast, gratitude is a more passive energy, a feeling that results from having been given something—knowing that you have been given the gift of life and reaching out to receive it joyously with both hands.

The relationship between love and gratitude may be similar to the relationship between sun and shade. If love is the sun, gratitude is the moon. If love is man, gratitude is woman.

So then what does it mean to say that the passive energy of the shade or gratitude is stronger than love? When I was thinking about this question, I stumbled upon an interesting concept, which became an important clue to answering the question concerning how we can and should live our lives.

What is the relationship between love and gratitude? For an answer to this question, we can use water as a model. A water molecule consists of two hydrogen atoms and one oxygen atom, represented by H_2O. If love and gratitude, like oxygen and hydrogen, were linked together in a ratio of 1 to 2, gratitude would be twice as large as love.

I suggest that having twice the amount of gratitude as love is the balance we should strive for. At a seminar, after I had mentioned this in my presentation, two young women came up to me and said, "We were very impressed. Weren't you saying that people have one mouth for speaking and two ears for listening?"

"That's right—that's absolutely right!" I exclaimed, and I knew that I had become a little wiser.

When we observe the natural world, we can see that the passive energy has greater strength. The fish of the sea produce enormous numbers of eggs, but not all of them hatch. Only a small portion reach the stage where they hatch, while the remaining eggs are offered as food to other creatures.

Have human beings lived in a ratio of two parts gratitude and one part love? I suspect that the exact opposite is true.

Of course, the grandeur of love cannot be denied, and most people do have a general understanding of the power of love. However, we have been raised in a culture where all our focus is placed on the energy of love, while the other side of the formula receives little attention.

The focus of the human race has been drawn away from that which cannot be seen, and towards the obvious physical world. And in order to make as much of this physical world our own as possible, we have cut down forests and fought back deserts in an effort to insure the supreme domination of our culture.

Such advancements by human society may indeed be the result of love—for our families and our countries—but as long as we continue to live our lives based on this strategy, there will be no end to conflict. The history of the twentieth century was the history of fighting and warfare.

Perhaps we are finally beginning to see that the direction we are moving in leads nowhere. We have sacrificed too much in order to secure the riches of life. Forests have been destroyed and clean water lost, and we have cut up and sold the earth itself.

What the world needs now is gratitude. We must begin by learning what it means to have enough. We need to feel gratitude for having been born on a planet so rich in nature, and gratitude for the water that makes our life possible. Do we really know how wonderful it is to be able to breathe a big breath of clean air?

If you open your eyes, you will see that the world is full of so much that deserves your gratitude.

When you have become the embodiment of gratitude, think about how pure the water that fills your body will be. When this happens, you yourself will be a beautiful, shining crystal of light.

CHAPTER FOUR

The World Will Change
in but a Moment

Do you know where you can obtain really
good water?

Perhaps at the foot of the Swiss Alps; or maybe at
the North or South pole? It's not hard nowadays to find
bottled water claiming to be the best in the world, but
can good water really be purchased?

Water is not simply about H_2O. No matter how
natural or pure the water you drink, without a pure
soul, it will not taste good.

Let me ask you: How clear is your soul? Are you
weighed down by trouble at work? What about family problems? Is your consciousness troubled? If it is,

then you may find that the water you drink tastes plain and dull.

After you've enjoyed participating in a sport or other exercise, water—even just tap water—tastes delicious and refreshing. In other words, it's what's inside you that counts the most.

I know it sounds like I'm saying that it's all in your mind, but what I'm actually trying to say is that when you drink water with a feeling of gratitude the water itself is physically different than when you drink the same water with clouded feelings in your soul.

Our emotions and feelings have an effect on the world moment by moment. If you send out words and images of creativity, then you will be contributing to the creation of a beautiful world. However, emitting messages of destruction, you contribute to the destruction of the universe.

If you become aware of this, you will no longer be able to speak words of anger to those around you, or blame others for your own mistakes and weaknesses. You have the capacity to change the world within a moment. All you must do is make a simple choice. *Are you going to choose a world of love and gratitude, or a tortured world filled with discontent and impoverishment?* The answer will depend on your attitude at this very moment.

According to the teachings of Buddhism, everything in the world is constantly changing, and nothing ever changes. Speaking from the principles of vibration, the energy of vibration must go on forever in continuous motion.

Understanding that everything exists in this one moment will give hope and light to your life. You no longer need to be troubled by the past, and can know that the future can be anything that you *will* it to be. You, as you are, in this very moment hold the key to everything.

If you want to see how much of an impact your consciousness can have on the world, I suggest that you conduct a little experiment by playing a game we'll call "cloud erasing." I want you to try to erase clouds using the power of your thoughts.

On a partially clear day, look up in the sky and target just one cloud, maybe one not too large. Your thoughts are very important in playing this game, and so it's important to believe that the cloud will disappear, but you shouldn't try too hard. Focusing too hard will actually have the effect of preventing your energy from being sent out.

When you are ready, imagine an invisible beam of energy being sent from your consciousness towards the cloud, breaking it into pieces. See in your mind how the laser-beam targets the entire cloud and not just one part.

Then say, in the past tense, "The cloud has disappeared"; at the same time, say to the energy (again in the past tense), "Thank you for doing that." If you follow these steps, I'm sure that the cloud will start to thin out and disappear in a matter of minutes.

As this shows, human consciousness can have an enormous impact on the world around us. Clouds consist of water in the gaseous state, and so it responds especially quickly to our will.

Traditionally speaking, anyone who says that consciousness has an effect on the physical world risks certain ostracization for being unscientific. However, science has progressed to a point where the failure to understand consciousness and the mind limits our understanding of much of the world around us.

Quantum mechanics, certain psychological theories (such as the flow talked about by Jung), and genetic engineering have all taught us that there is a world other than the one we know so well. You can't see this other world with your eyes, and you can't touch it with your fingers. It's a world in which time itself does not exist.

The famous quantum theorist David Bohm has called the world available to our senses the "explicate order," and the existence within, the "implicate order." He envisions that everything that exists in the explicate order has been enfolded in the implicate order, and each part of the explicate order includes all the information of the implicate order.

This may be difficult to understand, but what he is saying is that every part of the universe contains the information of *all* the parts of the universe. In other words, within an individual—and even within a single cell—exists all the information of the universe.

The information of the universe includes *time*. In other words, the fact that you exist in the here-and-now is included in the information of the universe, along with all present, past, and future information. So the changing of the entire world in a moment isn't just a fantasy.

But let's think about *this* moment for a moment. How can we interpret it using physical science? David Bohm explained that an aspect of the universe within is projected into each moment in time, creating the present. The next moment in time is also a projection of a different aspect, and so on. In other words, with each moment, a different world is being shown to us. However, one momentary world will have an impact on the next momentary world, and so it appears to us as one continuous world.

Based on this theory, the world is changing every moment, and being created anew. Our consciousness has a role to play in this creation of the world. If you become aware of this, I suspect that your life will never be the same.

I've talked about some complicated things, and may have caused some confusion. But if we reconsider crystals, it will help to answer many questions. This world is changing moment by moment, and water is the first to recognize the change.

I mentioned that I made a device for measuring vibration, and used it to better understand water. On the afternoon of the invasion of Iraq at the onset of the first Gulf War, I measured the vibration of the tap water in Tokyo, and found an unusually sharp increase in the values of vibrations produced by mercury, lead, aluminum, and other substances harmful to the human body. There seemed to be no apparent explanation for this; at first I suspected that there was something wrong with my equipment, but repeated measurements indicated otherwise. It wasn't until the following day, when I read the newspaper, that I made the connection. News of the start of the Gulf War covered the front page. It's been said that the weight of the bombs dropped on this first day of war was equivalent to all the bombs dropped throughout the Vietnam War.

In Japan, thousands of miles from the Middle East, I was able to measure the vibrations from harmful substances at almost the exact time that war broke out. You might ask, *Is this really possible?*

Of course, the harmful by-products of the bombs in the Middle East weren't immediately transported to Japan. However, the harmful vibrations of the bombs being dropped on one side of the earth did reach the corners of the earth immediately. These vibrations spread out beyond the limits of time and space.

I suspect that vibrations exist not in our three-dimensional world, and not in the unseen world of a different dimension, but in a middle world. When something occurs on the earth, in no matter what world, water is the first to detect it and relay this new information to us.

At the time of the Gulf War, I hadn't yet started taking photographs of crystals, but if I had taken photographs, I'm sure they would have been very interesting.

Let me give you one more example in which vibrations had an immediate impact on the physical world. In this case, the power of prayer was used to purify water.

At Fujiwara Dam in central Japan, we had a Shinto priest of the Shingon Sect named Houki Kato repeat an incantation. When I first met him, he showed me two photographs that made a lasting impression, and so I wanted to see for myself what was recorded in the photographs. One of the photographs had been taken before an incantation, and the other after; the second photograph showed a remarkable difference—the water was considerably clearer.

The power of the incantation had come from the *spirit of words*, and so it is possible that the energy from the *spirit of words* had purified the water in the lake. In order to verify this, I wanted to take photographs of crystals formed from water before and after such an incantation.

The priest stood on the edge of the lake and performed the incantation for about an hour, all of which I videotaped. After the incantation, the priest and I conversed; within fifteen minutes, my crew called me over.

"This is incredible! The water is getting clearer right in front of our eyes," someone said. And it was absolutely true. You could clearly see that the water was becoming more and more transparent as we looked at it. We were even able to make out the foliage at the bottom of the lake, which had been hidden by the cloudy water.

We next took photographs of crystals. The crystals made with water from before the incantation were distorted, and looked like the face of someone in great pain. But the crystals from water taken after the incantation were complete and grand. Within one hexagonal shape there was a smaller hexagonal shape, all enclosed by a halo-like pattern of light.

Of course, it did take some time after the incantation for the water to become clear, indicating that changes in substances that can be seen with the naked eye are somewhat gradual. But there is no doubt that the vibrations of prayer are relayed to nearby objects in an immediate way, affecting the nearby water. This was a physical phenomenon that can't be explained unless we accept that another world exists within the one we call our own.

But the story doesn't end there. A few days after this experiment, an incident was reported in the press. The body of a woman was found in the lake, and when I heard about this I remembered the crystals created from the water before the prayer, and remembered how the crystals had looked like a face in agony.

Perhaps through the crystals, the spirit of this woman was trying to tell us something. I would like to think that her suffering was alleviated in part by the incantation.

There is another world in addition to the one that we live in. When looking at our world from that world, we can see things that we cannot see now.

Dr. Rupert Sheldrake of England is a researcher who focuses on furthering the understanding of a new worldview, in association with this world that we cannot see. After receiving a doctorate in biochemistry from Cambridge University, he served as a lecturer in biochemistry and biology at Cambridge, while also serving as a Fellow of the Royal Society.

Dr. Sheldrake's theory is outlined in a book that he wrote more than twenty years ago, but the scientific journal *Nature* dismissed the book by saying that it should be burned. Despite this rejection, his theory reached the hearts of many, and research into his theory continues. What was it that drew so much attention?

It's often said that if something happens twice it will happen again. Perhaps you have found it strange that accidents and crimes tend to happen in series. Looking at history and social trends, you can see that over long periods of time, events do generally repeat themselves. How can we explain this strange repetition of events? Dr. Sheldrake attempted to use scientific means to find an answer.

Scientists normally approach objects that they can't see with their eyes by using reductionism to isolate a physical phenomenon. However, Dr. Sheldrake took an entirely different approach.

According to his theory, when the same thing repeats itself, a *morphic field* is formed, and resonance with this morphic field increases the likelihood that the event will happen again. A morphic field is not energy-based information, but more like a blueprint for building a house.

We can see this as an example of resonance theory. Dr. Sheldrake has proposed that events are also capable of resonating in the same way that sound resonates. He refers to the location where such events take place as the morphic field, and the phenomena of repeated similar events as *morphic resonance*.

Although his theory was quickly dismissed by *Nature*, the announcement of his theory was taken seriously by the more open-minded, resulting in serious discussion. There is no doubt that Dr. Sheldrake has departed from the existing paths laid out by science, but you have to admit that his theory goes a long way toward explaining mysteries that traditional science has been unable to deal with.

During typical discussions of such mysteries, the talk often turns to glycerin crystals. For the first forty or so years after glycerin was discovered, it was generally accepted that it didn't form crystals. Then one day at the beginning of the nineteenth century, a drum of glycerin en route from Vienna to London suddenly started to crystallize.

A short time later, in a completely different location, another batch of glycerin also crystallized. This crystallization began to spread, and now it is generally accepted that glycerin forms crystals when temperatures drop below 17°C (63°F).

So what should we make of this?

When the crystals first formed (for whatever reason), a morphic field was created, and eventually all glycerin, in compliance with the morphic field, started to form crystals. This type of phenomenon has occurred in many other substances as well. Despite all the randomness in the world, once a substance begins to form crystals, then it often becomes common for it to form crystals thereafter.

Not too many years ago, a television station in England decide to conduct a public experiment to see if they could test the validity of Dr. Sheldrake's theory of morphic resonance. They first prepared two paintings: both looked like random patterns, but within one was hidden the figure of a woman wearing a hat, and within the other a man with a mustache. The figures were designed such that it was impossible to see them.

The experiment took place in three steps. First, before the live program, a group of participants were asked to identify what they saw in the paintings. Second, during the program, the secret of the painting of the man with the mustache was revealed. Third, after the program, another group of participants, who weren't allowed to watch the program, were likewise asked to identify the paintings.

What do you think the results were? The second group did a far better job than the first in identifying the man with a mustache. The experimenters did their best to account for all possible factors, such as removing the data from viewers in countries other than England and Ireland, but the results still showed that the second did three times better than the first.

This experiment tells us that when someone becomes aware of something, other people also tend to become aware. It was the effect of the morphic field that led to the remarkable increase in correct responses.

According to Dr. Sheldrake, DNA isn't the only reason that people in the same family share similar features—morphic resonance also plays a part. Dr. Sheldrake's theory also helps us to understand so-called coincidences (referred to as "sychronicity"), and the phenomena of group consciousness (collective memory) and archetypal patterns.

The important thing about Dr. Sheldrake's theory is that once the morphic resonance has spread, it extends to all space and all time. In other words, if a morphic field is formed, it will have an instantaneous impact on all other locations, resulting in an instantaneous worldwide change.

When I first heard about Dr. Sheldrake's theory, I couldn't contain my interest, because my research into water crystals was nothing less than an attempt to express the resonance of the morphic field in a way that can be seen with the naked eye.

When I first attempted to take photographs of crystals, I had no success at all for the first two months, but once I was able to capture the first photograph, other researchers also started to succeed. Perhaps this is also a result of morphic resonance.

I first learned about Dr. Sheldrake's work from a bestselling book in Japan, called *Why Does That Occur?*

by Eiichi Hojiro, but I became truly interested when I saw Sheldrake in a television documentary called *Six Scientists of Interest*. Four years later, as luck would have it, I had the opportunity to meet Dr. Sheldrake during a lecture tour of Europe. A friend who attended the seminar happened to know Sheldrake's wife, and so I found myself invited to their home in London.

I was pleased to learn that he already knew about my research into water crystals; he said, "At least once every week I get a letter from someone telling me about you." I had many questions for Dr. Sheldrake, but he was also extremely interested in my work, and as it turned out he had as many or more questions for me.

He also shared the following with me:

I have conducted research into living organisms and their behavior but not water; and so I'm not that familiar with water. However, it's likely that in the future there will be connections between my research and your research into water crystals.

The area that I'm most interested in is the effect that observation has on the observed. There are people who know when someone is looking at them from behind. I want to do research to try and express this in a statistical way.

There's a risk that the documentation on this research will be subjective, so I'm wondering if we can't use water in the experiment. I'm going to try to take photographs of crystals and see how water changes under various conditions, such as when the water is ignored, and when it is observed by people with special talents, normal people, and then extremely evil people.

This sounded remarkably similar to the experiment in which the rice in the ignored bottle rotted faster than the rice in the bottles exposed to "Thank you" and "You fool." When I told him about this experiment, he became even more interested, and he suggested that if I tested the effect of just looking at water, it would be easier to get results than using rice (which involves the complicated growth process of microbes).

Dr. Sheldrake currently has a strong interest in the phenomena of telepathy. He conducted an experiment to find out if dogs showed a response when their masters started to head home. Using video equipment to make observations, he has been able to verify this phenomenon in more than two hundred cases.

I would like to pass on to you a message that I received from Dr. Sheldrake:

Our lives are made possible by the movement of an unseen energy. Therefore, I would hope that we'll always be aware of this and pay attention to those around us and the things going on around us. This is something that is very important. This is because the act of looking at something has an effect on it. Everyone seems to be aware of this, but we don't put it into practice. In the home, parents need to pay attention to their children. It's the same thing.

Focusing your attention—on anything—serves as an expression of love. Dr. Sheldrake is on the leading edge of this study of the impact of consciousness on objects, and so his words come with special significance.

If we combine the lessons that water teaches us with the theories proposed by Dr. Sheldrake, we go a long way toward unlocking the many mysteries of our world. Each one of us has a magical ability to change the world. We have all been granted the power of creation by God. If we use this power to the maximum, we will be able to change the world in but a moment.

For people who see no end to their worries and suffering, this perspective should come as considerable comfort. You—yes *you*—have the ability to change the world!

Everything in the world is linked. Whatever you are doing now is being done by someone else at the same time. So what type of morphic field should we be interested in creating? Are we creating fields of pain and viciousness, or are we creating a world filled with love and gratitude?

Whenever you sit in front of water and send out messages of love and gratitude, somewhere in the world, someone is being filled with love and gratitude. You don't need to go anywhere. The water right in front of you is linked to the all the water in the world. The water you're looking at will resonate with water everywhere, and your message of love will reach the souls of all the people of the world.

We can cover the world in love and gratitude. This will become a glorious morphic field that will change the world. It's not about time and space; now, here, wonderful and marvelous things are possible.

Note: The following color photographs on pages 101 to 132 are referred to in chapter 5, page 133.

Water shown photographs of natural scenery

We placed a jar of water on photographs of beautiful scenery, then photographed the crystals that formed. We see here how water responded to the photographs.

Sun

The crystal, resulting from exposure to the photograph of the sun, is large and beautiful, not unlike the sun itself.

Mt. Fuji

The symbolic mountain of Japan. Perhaps incidentally, the crystal looks as though it were being enveloped by the first rays of morning.

Rocky Mountains

The tips of the Rocky Mountains, the backbone of North America, are covered in glaciers. The crystal also looks like it is encased in snow.

Victoria Falls

An enormous waterfall in Zimbabwe. As if to represent the plunging water, the crystal is formed of broad columns.

Stonehenge

Stonehenge, the giant stone structure in England, is built on a site of high energy, and the crystal also appears full of energy.

Coral reef

All three of the crystals are unique, but formed of
smaller detailed crystals. Their form and color does
seem somewhat similar to the beautiful and life-filled
corals of the ocean.

African savanna

The crystals seem to represent the finite and nurturing foliage of the savanna.

Rainforest, Southeast Asia

This rainforest, overflowing with life, protects an ecological system dating back millions of years. The crystal
appears to be formed by a steady and finite balance.

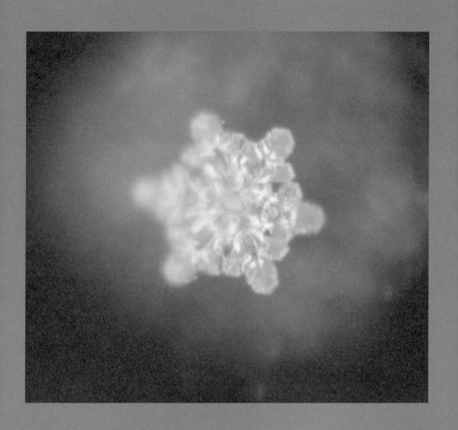

Machu Picchu, Peru

Small yet beautiful like a diamond, the crystal reminds us
of the glory of the Inca Empire.

A pool in Yellowstone

This is a beautiful, clear-blue pool in Yellowstone
National Park. The crystal is indicative of the stunning
color of a fine jewel.

Heitate Shrine

The oldest in Japan, the Heitate Shrine was mostly
unknown until a few years ago when this area was identi-
fied as the location of mythological stone gates. The
crystals look like two gates being opened.

Water exposed to music of the world

The music from the various cultures of the world has similarly various rhythms and melodies. Water captures these characteristics and reveals them to us through crystals.

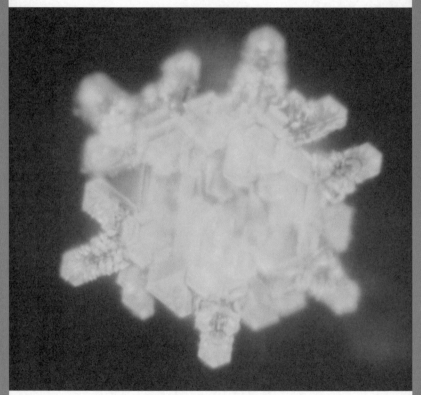

Tibetan Buddhist chant

The detailed interlocking crystal indicates strength, somewhat like the temples of Tibet.

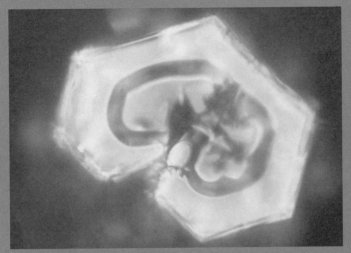

Arirang (Korean folk song)

Ketjak (music of Bali)

Arirang is a sad song about lovers being separated, and the crystal seems to indicate a broken heart. Ketjak produced a detailed crystal, making us see why music can heal the soul.

Brazilian music

Both crystals are in the shape of stars. They seem to be telling us that moving your body and singing in a loud voice serves to strengthen your immune system.

Argentine tango

Both crystals formed unique pair crystals, indicating a dancing couple. It's fun just to look at them!

Gospel music

The form seems to represent the desires of people to resonate with God. Music from around the world has the capacity to heal.

Polka from Czechoslovakia

Beer-keg polka from Austria

Czechoslovakia and Austria, although distant from each other, form similar-looking crystals.

Yodeling from Austria

Tyrolean lullaby from Austria

These crystals are also unique. The top crystal reminds one of a mouth yodeling, while in the center of the lower crystal we can see what appears to be a child.

Tap water of the world

Due to water treatment methods, it's difficult to form crystals using tap water from almost anywhere in the world. Perhaps it is time that we cooperate, and learn from each other how to better care for our water.

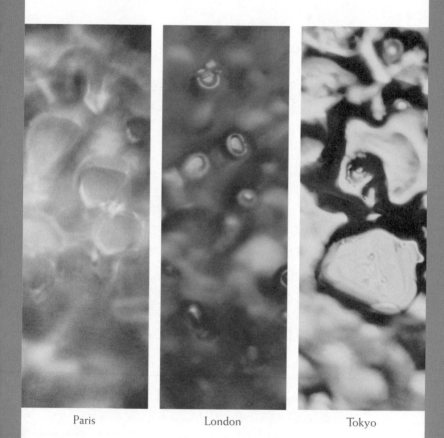

Paris   London   Tokyo

Water crystals fail to form, a result of using substances that harm the natural life-giving force of nature.

Rome

Venice

Bern

Even in Venice, the city of water, crystals failed to form in the tap water. Crystals just barely formed from the water of Bern in Switzerland.

Washington D.C.

New York

Surprisingly, the water of some large cities in the
United States formed beautiful crystals. This may be the
result of efforts to protect water, such as the use of
cedar tanks in Manhattan.

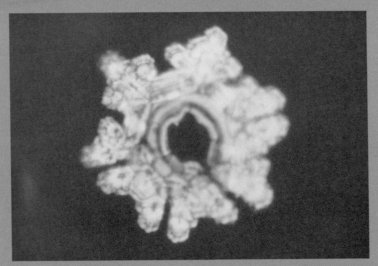

Vancouver

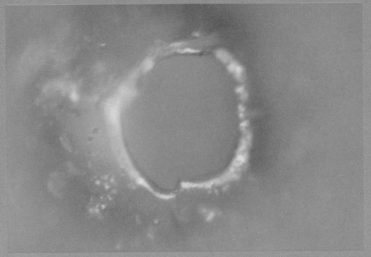

Sydney

The water from Vancouver produced relatively complete crystals, perhaps because of the bountiful supply of water in the Rocky Mountains. The water from Sydney resulted in a surprisingly deformed crystal.

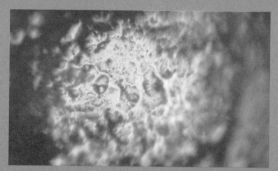

Bangkok

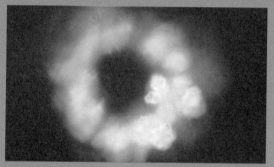

Hong Kong

Macao

It seems that the water of Asia is at least as bad as that of many cities in Europe and America.

Buenos Aires

Manaus

These crystals are from two cities in South America.
Manaus is located on the banks of the bountiful
Amazon River, in Brazil. Beautiful crystals came from
the water of Buenos Aires.

The beautiful glory of natural water

Well-formed and jewellike crystals were formed from natural water from glaciers, springs, and rivers.

Spring water from Saijo, Hiroshima

This detailed crystal looks like a beautiful ornament made of silver. Some of the best-tasting water (and sake) in Japan comes from Saijo.

125

Sanbu-ichi Yusui spring water from Kita-koma-gun, Yamanashi prefecture

The crystal seems to shine like the sun. Melted snow runs off Yatsugatake peaks and seeps into the ground to emerge as spring water. This is an expression of the true beauty of nature.

Spring water from Chuzenji Lake

Spring water from Chuzenji Lake, treated with chlorine

The top crystal was made using spring water at a hotel on the banks of Chuzenji Lake. Chlorinating the water, at the instructions of the local government, resulted in a marked change, as shown in the bottom crystal.

Lourdes spring water

Fontana di Trevi

The water of Lourdes spring in France appears similar to the crystal formed from water shown the word "angel." The crystal from the Fontana di Trevi in Italy is unique, and appears similar to the gold coins that people throw in the fountain.

Tasmanian spring water

New Zealand groundwater

Spring water from a diamond-rich area of Tasmania
produced crystals that look like little diamonds. The
groundwater of New Zealand also created beautiful
crystals.

South Pole

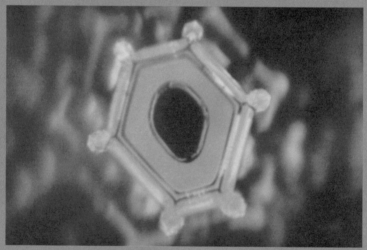

Columbia Glacier, Canada

At the South Pole, snow from thousands of years has
become hardened, resulting in the sturdy-looking crystal at the top. The water for both crystals was made
from snow on the surface, and so it did include a small
amount of modern-day pollution.

Tenderfoot Lake, Wisconsin

A lake near Mount Myohyang, North Korea

I gathered the water from Tenderfoot Lake at the bottom of a ravine. The water from North Korea was the first I received from that country, and the result was a beautiful and fanciful crystal.

Lake Brienz

Lake Maggiore

These crystals are from water that I gathered myself in Switzerland. It's not surprising that the crystals came from Switzerland, the water capital of Europe.

CHAPTER FIVE

~~~~~~~~~~~~

A Smile That Fills the World

Wanting as many people as possible to know about the wonderful mysteries of the universe as revealed through water crystals, I published the collection of my water crystal photographs in Japan, but I actually got a larger response from Europe. It seems that a ripple effect in people's souls resulted, which spread at a speed far faster than I could have imagined.

What could it be that caught the interest of so many people in so many different countries? I think that when a person looks at the photographs of water crystals, a physical change takes place in the water within that person's body. Water has a message for the world: *The world is linked together by love and gratitude.*

Love and gratitude are fundamental principles of nature. At the end of its long journey through the cosmos, water arrived on the earth with love and gratitude in its bosom. This love and gratitude created the first inkling of life, and then provided the tender nurturing required for growth. Looking at the water crystal photographs awakens a primeval memory contained deep within the water in each of our cells.

The message of water is love and gratitude.

Review the photographs of crystals found on pages 101–132 of this book. These images reflect our beautiful world. The photographs indicate the change in water resulting from scenery and music from around the world, and include a comparison between tap water and natural water.

As mentioned in the first chapter, the world first learned about my work through my first collection of photographs of water crystals. This was made possible by the efforts of Shizuko Ouwehand, a Japanese woman with Dutch citizenship, who now serves as my interpreter.

Through the introduction of a common acquaintance, Shizuko visited my office less than a month after this collection of photographs was first published in Japan, and I showed her a copy of the book.

The moment she looked at the photographs, I could tell that she was impressed. Right then and there, she purchased seventy-seven copies, which she sent to friends and acquaintances in the Netherlands, Switzerland, Germany, the United States, Australia, and other countries.

Not long after sending out the books, she started getting a flood of responses in return. It was as if the crystals were exactly what so many people were looking for—what these difficult times that we live in require. Shizuko subsequently invited me to give a presentation at a small annual seminar that she holds in Zurich, Switzerland, entitled "Looking for Human Jewels."

A week after this event, there was to be a major annual gathering; with Shizuko's assistance I would have the opportunity to lecture before several reporters, and to be interviewed for articles in a few magazines. The result would be an enormous wave of interest in and understanding of my work.

One of the people behind this major event was Manuela Kihm, another person who saw the collection of photographs and became enchanted. She sent the following message:

> I have two children, and I know that there's a
> completely different effect when you speak to

children with love and when you just order them. It's the difference between "Let's do it,'" and "Do it." I also clearly understand that this is felt in each one of our cells.

In our daily lives, water crystals teach us very important things. Every day we are surrounded by magnetic fields. We find it impossible to live without computers. But we can clearly see that there is a great difference between being unaware of the risk of magnetic fields and being aware and careful. I was very impressed.

After seeing the photographs, Manuela invited me to give a seminar that she would organize. She first talked to the environmental agency of a small town called Sanglant about a lecture on the theme of water and the environment, but they said they couldn't help because the topic was too delicate. She then turned to those more open to spiritual matters, and gathered groups of people who had a desire to explore that which cannot be seen with the naked eye. All those who heard about the water crystals were visibly impressed and inspired.

Thanks to Manuela's efforts, in the course of a week I gave presentations in three cities in Switzerland, and I returned to Japan knowing that there were vast numbers of people with a desire to learn more about what I was doing.

Manuela's first invitation was followed by many others, and wherever I have spoken on the topic of water crystals, the response has been marvelous. I have had the opportunity to make many trips to Europe to give lectures and presentations at halls overflowing with people with a personal and professional interest in water.

The ensuing articles in magazines led to further interest abroad, and as more and more people showed interest in the collection of photographs, I was flooded with requests to give lectures and presentations.

Information about my work spread from Europe to the United States, where I was invited to speak at Harvard, and also at a "free school" in the suburbs of Boston, attended by children who did not fit into the American society stained by guns, drugs, and violence. It was probably this sensitivity of the students that made them more receptive to information about water crystals. I'm quite sure that the students left with the realization that saying unkind words causes damage to water as well as to other people. I imagine with a smile that they returned home that day and told their parents not to say things like "Do your homework!" or "Clean your room!"

But this is just one more aspect of the resonance phenomenon. As people who have had their tender souls damaged in some way learn about water crystals, the message of water spreads ever more quickly around the world.

Perhaps we can also say that this is the result of people searching for answers during these troubled times. I have no doubt that water crystals will become a common focal point for people all over the world who are trying to make sense of chaos.

My visits to Germany, Switzerland, the Netherlands, England, France, Italy, Canada, and the United States have given me the opportunity to meet and correspond with many others around the world who are also conducting research into water. Perhaps because water is so mysterious, the approaches are varied and unconventional.

All this interest in water means that symposiums and other gatherings are always being held around the world, making me quite busy—sometimes too busy. The symposium in Switzerland has since been held twice more in Lucerne, and it is likely to continue to grow and become more international as time goes by. I have also participated in symposiums in Australia and England.

I first wondered how much interest there would be in water in Europe and other countries, but now I know that other countries have as much or more interest than Japan. I remember hearing about a group of Japanese visiting Zurich Lake. The lake was so beautiful that one of the participants asked the Swiss tour guide, "Why isn't there any trash at all around?" The guide, who took it for granted that the lake would be clean, didn't know quite how to reply, and instead asked the Japanese, "Why do you ask such a question?"

Wherever I go, I take slides of the water crystal photographs, and then I show audiences the crystals formed from their own local water. When they hear my message and see the slides, Europeans are visibly surprised and impressed. Such forthright responses indicate that they have a high consciousness concerning water.

However, my research is limited when I make crystals in Japan, and so people have requested that I open a research facility in Europe. In response I have begun to talk about a concept that has been floating around in my head for a long time.

The concept is grand and unique—I want to create a research facility that is itself in the shape of a hexagonal water crystal. The laboratory for studying water crystals will be located at the center, and six other laboratories will be located around the center to study other subjects and fields of science: physics and mathematics, biology and medicine, astronomy and oceanography, philosophy and religion, and chemistry and engineering. Each of the labs will focus on 18 categories of research, for a total of 108.

I have been thinking about this for a long time, prompted when I started to think about why the environment of the earth is in such a bad state, why people are so confused, and why our civilization is such as it is. Pondering these questions led me to the conclusion that it is a result of the combination of, first, pride and corruption in the scientific community, and second, those in authority consciously allowing and encouraging the formation of such a society.

Of course, there are scientists who have their own will, and work according to their own consciousness. However, when we consider the condition of society, we realize that there are really very few who have conducted their activities with a mind to perpetuating the human race and cleansing this planet that we occupy.

This does not describe, for example, scientists at the beck and call of those in authority in Japan who insist that water must be tainted with chlorine, resulting in an overall decay of society.

Of course, scientists aren't the only ones responsible for the problem. The foundations of society have become so weak that it is no longer possible for a handful of scientists to change the deplorable direction in which we are headed.

How can we change direction, and do something to significantly improve the depressing state of affairs that permeates the scientific community? I think we must start by changing the environment and systems related to the scientific community.

In the laboratory that I have in mind, the local community will come together to support scientists, who will focus on their own field and also interact with scientists of other interests, giving them a wide perspective from which to structure their courses of research. The community will also help secure the necessary financing and other assistance that individual researchers are currently unable to obtain on their own. I expect that the result will be discoveries and advances that will truly contribute to the future of the earth and humankind.

I have an image of the researchers gathering at the central cafeteria for discussion during their morning and midday meals, and in the evening announcing the results of their research.

Of course, there are a great many obstacles that must be overcome to make this dream a reality, but I now feel that the first step has been taken.

No matter what your intentions, announcing them is an important step. I can say this with confidence based on many years of experience in business. From the time when I was a child, I was always telling people what I was thinking and what I wanted to do, and I was constantly being told that I talked too much. But the simple act of saying something is a way to gather energy towards you. Especially when you say something to other people, energy flows in your direction and helps you to achieve your aims.

If you express your intentions, the realization of those intentions will follow. Of course, I'm not proposing that you make irresponsible statements—it's important to say what you really feel inside. Your word is your promise, so when you say something you must have the determination to commit yourself. Letting other people know your intentions also often leads to the arrival of required assistance from unexpected sources.

Words have their individual and unique vibrational frequencies, and we've already seen how words have energy that influences the universe. The words from your mouth have a power of their own that influences the entire world. We can even say that the words that teach us about nature are the words of the Creator.

I know a man who has proven the power and benefits of words, using his own body. Nobuo Shioya is a man who I am proud to call my master. He is 101 years old, but his back is straight and he appears strong and healthy to anyone who sees him. Even now, he stands for one or two hours to give lectures several times a year. He also practices his golf swing every day, and goes to the course once a week. His ability to maintain his health is nothing less than miraculous.

Master Shioya says that his secret for health is his own unique breathing method. This method involves breathing in until air fills the lungs, providing oxygen to the entire body, while thinking about the energy of the universe gathering around him and providing him with invigorating energy. This method also indicates to us the power of affirmations. Master Shioya recommends that at the end of his breathing exercise, you say the following affirmation: "The infinite power of the universe *will* be concentrated and bring true peace to the world." This statement is a type of prayer, but what is important is his strong determination expressed by the word *will*.

According to Master Shioya, there are ghostly particles that cannot be seen by the means of today's science because they exist on the border between the third and fourth dimensions. Words spoken with determination have a strong power that gathers these ghost particles, making it possible to accomplish things in the three-dimensional world.

In September 1999, I had the opportunity to actually feel the power of words as expressed by Master Shioya. On this day, approximately 350 people had gathered on the banks of Lake Biwa, Japan's largest lake. I had gathered the group together in an attempt to clean the lake. There's an old saying in Japan that when the water of Lake Biwa is clean, the water of all

Japan will be clean. Another purpose of the gathering was to pray for peace for the entire world as we entered the new century.

Under the direction of Master Shioya, who was 97 at the time, this large crowd joined forces in an affirmation for world peace that brought our voices and hearts together. Our chants could be heard around the entire lake, and there was a special feeling that made our spines tingle.

Just a month after this event took place, a strange thing happened to Lake Biwa. The newspapers reported that the putrid algae that appeared each year and caused an unbearable stench had not appeared that year.

If you don't understand the principles of the *spirit of words*, this happening will indeed seem strange, but we know that this spirit of words has the power to influence all of existence and change the world almost immediately. I have no doubt that the spirit of words generated from the determined prayers for world peace had the affect of cleansing the water in the lake in only a matter of moments. Another important point is the fact that 350 people gathered and chanted together. The combined will of so many people acted as a force to change the universe.

I sometimes use Einstein's theory of relativity ($E = MC^2$) to explain this principle. This formula has an

additional important meaning. The general understanding is that $E = MC^2$ means "energy equals mass
times the speed of light squared." However, we can also
interpret C as *consciousness* instead of the speed of light.
Since M represents mass, we can interpret it as the
number of people consciously focused.

This interpretation was taught to me by Professor
Hoang Van Duc, a scholar of psychoimmunology born
in Vietnam. More than ten years ago, when I invited
him to attend a seminar I was holding in Japan, he
mentioned in casual conversation that the "C" of $E =
MC^2$ referred not to the speed of light, but to con-
sciousness. This perspective made a deep and lasting
impression on me; later, when I was thinking about
vibration and how people should live their lives, I suddenly recalled those words.

Almost a century has passed since Einstein announced
this formula to the world. There is no way of knowing
if Einstein himself considered the possibility of C rep-
resenting consciousness, but since everything in the
universe is relative, you can't say that it is a mistake to
see the formula in this new way.

It is said that people make use of at most 30 percent
of their abilities, but if we can increase our abilities by
just 1 percent, then this amount, according to the formula, will be squared, doubling the amount of energy.
If people around the world were all to increase their

consciousness at the same time, the difference in energy would be enormous.

If we fill our lives with love and gratitude for all, this consciousness will become a wonderful power that will spread throughout the world. And *this* is what water crystals are trying to tell us.

I have just described how the earnest prayer and thoughts of a group of people were able to cleanse the water of a lake, but those who have seen the photographs of the crystals should not be surprised by the fact that our thoughts have the ability to change water. Several years back, I had a desire to take another step toward establishing the scientific foundations for my theories, but I wasn't quite sure how to go about it. I found the hint I was looking for one day when I happened to open the newspaper. The headline that captured my eye spoke of the ability to use ultrasound to decompose dioxin in water. The article reported on the development of a technology to expose water to 1,100 kHz of ultrasound, creating tiny air bubbles that decompose dioxin and other deadly toxins when they burst.

When I read this article, I couldn't contain my excitement. I knew that I had finally found a way to analyze the energy from the spirit of words. When the 350 people gathered on the banks of Lake Biwa to chant and pray for world peace, it is possible that they also created 2,000 kHz of ultrasound. Ultrasound is in the range that cannot be detected by the human ear, so they didn't create this ultrasound with their voices. However, it is possible, based on the principle of resonance of tuning with the same sounds in different octaves, that the conditions were right for creating ultrasound.

It must be said that the power of the spirit of words is indeed marvelous, but if we combined the ultrasound technology for purifying water with water vibration technology, the effect on water would be much greater.

For example, after water polluted with industrial chemicals is treated with ultrasound, it could then be treated in a second process with vibration. When polluted water is exposed to 1,100 kHz of ultrasound, the chemicals are decomposed when the air bubbles break up; although the toxins have decomposed, they are still there. To rid the water of these toxins, it is necessary to expose the water to information with the opposite vibrational frequency of the toxins.

Using just one of these two methods may not be sufficient, but by combining them it may be possible to completely rid the water of any harmful pollutants. And it might just be possible to use this same combined technology to get rid of the harmful substances within our own bodies.

What does the future hold for research into water crystals? To answer this question, we need to think more about how much scientific recognition this research will receive. When I show the photographs at my lectures abroad, I'm bombarded with a variety of questions. For example: What are the differences in crystal formation when the water is exposed to digital versus analog music? What about live music? In order to answer such questions, I need to continue research and conduct more tests under a variety of circumstances.

Another important issue is test repeatability. Many times we have seen that crystal formation depends on the observer's consciousness. When water samples are put into Petri dishes—we usually make fifty samples—the resulting crystals differ, depending on how the water is handled and on the thoughts of the researcher. And the condition of the fifty samples of water changes moment by moment.

It may be practically impossible to control all of these factors to the point where we can say scientifically that all conditions are equal. However, our approach has been to get as close to these conditions as possible, by using the most accurate scientific methods available.

Our efforts include the use of blinds to remove the possibility of change from the researchers' thoughts. We do this because we don't want the thought that the water being told "Thank you" will produce a more beautiful crystal than that being told "You fool" to have an impact on the results. We label the sample dishes with letters of the alphabet, and don't reveal which water is which until after the results have been seen. We hope that this method will remove the effect of the researchers' thoughts as much as possible.

For each of the fifty dishes, we make graphs showing the number of crystals in each dish that are considered beautiful, hexagonal, incomplete, and so on. For each pattern, we establish a coefficient, and give number values to the crystals. This gives us a clear picture of the characteristics of the crystals in each individual sample, and we then can classify the samples into the categories of beautiful, hexagonal, and so forth. Then we choose one crystal to photograph that best represents the characteristics of that particular sample.

Water crystals change depending on the thoughts and even the health of the observers. To account for this, we have several experienced researchers observe the samples. The intention of our research is to use these methods to discover the messages that are contained in this most delicate of messengers.

Perhaps one area in which research into water crystals can be most helpful is the prediction of earthquakes. It is believed that water is capable of detecting a forthcoming earthquake earlier than any other substance.

I envision a time when water samples will be taken from groundwater daily, and by observing the changes in crystal formation, we will detect changes in the earth's crust. When an earthquake takes place, we can compare photographs of crystals made from water taken before and after the earthquake. By accumulating data on the crystals leading up to the earthquake, we will be able to find similarities, and ultimately be able to use this information to predict future earthquakes.

Having lost my grandparents and an aunt on my mother's side in a terrible earthquake in 1923, and considering the pain and destruction caused by the earthquake that hit Kobe in 1995, I can personally say that being able to use water crystals to predict earthquakes would be an enormous contribution to humankind.

It is also quite possible that this technology could someday be used to predict other forms of destruction, such as storms, floods, epidemics, and even the planning of a secret attack from a hostile country.

I am also working on finding a way for everyone, with or without scientific equipment and knowledge, to take photographs of crystals. With the use of new materials, it appears that this will be possible in the not-too-distant future. We are looking at super-thermoconductive materials that are twenty times more efficient than normal thermoconductive materials, making it possible to freeze water at room temperature;

it will no longer be necessary to take photographs in a special room cooled to −5°C (23°F). Researchers are now developing a device based on this technology that will allow anyone to take crystal photographs almost anywhere.

I suspect that water crystal technology will in the future be shared by all humankind. However, this could also be a double-edged sword. Used correctly, water has the potential to bring unlimited glory and happiness to humankind, but such technology can also be used for gain, or to cause harm.

Our bodies are mostly water, and so life cannot continue without it. But we cannot forget that water also has the potential to wash away civilization and cause destruction. It all depends on what's in our souls. The human soul has the potential to bring happiness to the world, but also to bring pain. This is a fact that water crystals clearly reveal.

So how can we go about finding our path in life? I have constantly stressed the importance of love and gratitude. Gratitude is the creator of a heart filled with love. Love leads the feelings of gratitude in the right direction. As the water crystals show us, gratitude and love can spread throughout the world.

We all have an important mission: To make water clean again, and to create a world that is easy and healthy to live in. In order to accomplish our mission, we must first make sure that our hearts are clear and unpolluted.

Over the centuries, humankind has constantly robbed from the earth, and left it ever more polluted—the history of which is recorded by water. Now, water is beginning to speak to us. Through water crystals, it is telling us what we need to know.

Starting today, we must begin to carve out a new history. Water is carefully and quietly watching the direction that we take—the direction that *you* take at this very moment—and watching over us all.

I only ask that you listen to and absorb what water has to say—to all of humankind, and to you.

EPILOGUE

I sincerely hope that we can continue this wonderful discovery of water, and of the universe.

When I first heard that water constantly continues to arrive on the earth from the distant reaches of the universe, I was filled with wonderment. I began to think that if water continued to arrive at this pace, the earth would soon be flooded.

From ancient times, the human race has constantly been subject to damage and destruction caused by water. Almost all cultures of the world have a story of a great flood, and there is even scientific evidence that indicates that the earth was once covered in water. We cannot completely discount Noah and the great flood, and the tales of the civilization of Atlantis and the Mu continent lost to the sea.

The saying that history repeats itself is ultimately true, and so even now there exists the risk that water will arrive from space and once again cover our planet. This event may still be a thousand or ten thousand years in the future, but perhaps it is not too early to take action to ward off this disaster. Even now we frequently hear about floods in all parts of the world.

But once, when I found myself fretting about this possibility, another completely different thought came to me. Everything that exists in the universe is parallel. The micro world is a faithful reproduction of the macro world, and the universe is an enormous mandala (which means "circle" in Sanskrit). This way of thinking leads us to the conclusion that everything that takes place in the universe also takes place within our own bodies.

The human body requires the circulation of water, and we can conclude that this is what the universe also requires. If large volumes of water flow in only one direction, toward the earth, the circulation of water in the universe will ultimately come to a standstill. Water arrives on the earth and then ultimately returns to the far reaches of the universe on an unending marvelous journey. The water on this planet will someday set off on the outer leg of its journey into the cosmos.

But what does the fact that water is constantly arriving on the earth mean for us? Perhaps the earth is not the only destination for these lumps of water. But while there may be other stopovers, no other planet we know about has the necessary conditions required to pool water. If we compare the solar system to the human body, I suspect that the earth plays the role of the liver.

Each day, your liver filters two hundred liters of water and sends this purified water to the other organs in your body. Considering this, it's not hard to imagine that the earth plays the vital role of purifying the water circulating in the solar system, and then returning it to the universe.

Then whose responsibility is it to purify this water that has arrived on the earth? It is ours, humankind's. And this is because we are ourselves water. Having been born here, we all have the responsibility to purify the water on the earth.

As I ponder the long and marvelous journey that water takes through the universe, I find myself thinking about such things as the origin and future of humankind. But if we consider that we are water, then the answer to many of these mysteries becomes clear. Water makes up 70 percent of our bodies, and there is little doubt that the information in the water goes a long way in the formation of our personalities.

I have often heard cases of people injured in automobile or other accidents, who, while receiving blood transfusions, saw images of places they had never been, or had memories of a past that wasn't theirs. Sometimes transfusions have even been known to cause a change in personality.

It could be that the events we experience throughout our lives become memories recorded by water, which remain in our bodies, and may be what we call the soul.

There are still many questions left unanswered about the soul, rebirths, and the existence of spirits, but I suspect that the day will someday come when many of these questions will be answered by scientific means—using water.

Where does our soul come from? We have seen the possibility that it comes from the distant universe, carried by water.

So we ask next, what is in store for the soul? Since we are water itself, some day all our memories of experiences on this planet will be launched into space. And our responsibility before this happens is to become pure water on this earth.

To make this possible, we must first and foremost live life to the fullest. Our consciousness is what will purify water, and through this we send messages of beauty and strength to all life.

Wouldn't it be wonderful if we could cover the world in the most beautiful of water crystals?

How do we go about this? The answer is love and gratitude. I'd like to ask you to take another look at the beauty of the crystals. If all the people of the world can have love and gratitude, the pristine beauty of the earth will once again return.

We live our short lives on this planet and then we set out on a journey into the universe. I'm not sure how this process works, but we can leave this up to the laws of the universe. Of course, when we make this journey we will not be in our current physical form, but in the form of water or mist.

When my soul is ready to set out on its journey to the cosmos, I fully intend to call out to everyone and say, "We're off to see the universe! Let's go to Mars!"

ABOUT THE AUTHOR

Masaru Emoto was born in Yokohama in July, 1943. He is a graduate of the Yokohama Municipal University's department of humanities and sciences, with a focus on International Relations. In 1986 he established the IHM Corporation in Tokyo. In October of 1992 he received certification from the Open International University as a Doctor of Alternative Medicine. Subsequently he was introduced to the concept of micro-cluster water in the United States, and Magnetic Resonance Analysis technology. The quest thus began to discover the mystery of water.

Dr. Emoto undertook extensive research into water around the planet, not so much as a scientific researcher but more from the perspective of an original thinker. At length he realized that it was in the frozen crystal form that water showed us its true nature. He continues with this experimentation, and has written a variety of well-received books in Japanese, as well as the seminal *Messages from Water*, published bilingually. He is married to Kazuko Emoto who shares his passion and is head of Kyoikusha, the publishing arm of his company. They have three children.

Masaru Emoto's self published books, *The Message from Water volumes 1 and 2*, are available in English with Japanese subtitles from Source Books & Sacred Spaces.

To order contact:
Source Books & Sacred Spaces
PO Box 292231
Nashville, TN 37229-2231
(800) 637-5222 or (615) 773-7652
Fax: (615) 773-7016
www.sacredspaces.org
mail@sacredspaces.org

Other Books from
Beyond Words Publishing, Inc.

The Power of Appreciation
The Key to a Vibrant Life
Authors: Noelle C. Nelson, Ph.D.
and Jeannine Lemare Calaba, Psy.D.
$14.95, softcover

Research confirms that when people feel appreciation, good things happen to their minds, hearts, and bodies. But appreciation is much more than a feel-good mantra. It is an actual force, an energy that can be harnessed and used to transform our daily life—relationships, work, health and aging, finances, crises, and more. *The Power of Appreciation* will open your eyes to the fabulous rewards of conscious, proactive appreciation. Based on a five-step approach to developing an appreciative mind-set, this handbook for living healthier and happier also includes tips for overcoming resistance and roadblocks, research supporting the positive effects of appreciation, and guidelines for creating an Appreciators Group.

Forgiveness
The Greatest Healer of All
Author: Gerald G. Jampolsky, M.D.
Foreword: Neale Donald Walsch
$12.95, softcover

Forgiveness: The Greatest Healer of All is written in simple, down-to-earth language. It explains why so many of us find it difficult to forgive and why holding on to grievances is really a decision to suffer. The book describes what causes us to be unforgiving and how our minds work to justify this. It goes on to point out the toxic side effects of being unforgiving and the havoc it can play on our bodies and on our lives. But above all, it leads us to the vast benefits of forgiving.

The author shares powerful stories that open our hearts to the miracles which can take place when we truly believe that no one needs to be excluded from our love. Sprinkled throughout the book are Forgiveness Reminders that may be used as daily affirmations supporting a new life free of past grievances.

The Art of Thank You
Crafting Notes of Gratitude
Author: Connie Leas
$14.95, hardcover

While reminding us that a little gratitude can go a long way, this book distills the how-tos of thank-yous. Part inspirational, part how-to, *The Art of Thank You* will rekindle the gratitude in all of us and inspire readers to pick up a pen and take the time to show thanks. It stresses the healing power that comes from both giving and receiving thanks and provides practical, concrete, and inspirational examples of when to write a thank-you note and what that note should include. With its appealing and approachable style, beautiful gift presentation, charming examples, and real-life anecdotes, *The Art of Thank You* has the power to galvanize readers' resolve to start writing their all-important thank-you notes.

Summit Strategies
Secrets to Mastering the Everest in Your Life
Author: Gary P. Scott
$13.95, softcover

Picture your hands raised in a victory pose. No one but you, enjoying your moment, your victory lap, your knockout, your achievement, your crowning glory—your EVEREST!

From wherever you stand right now, *Summit Strategies* can help you reach your own personal summit. Through riveting accounts of lessons learned on the world's most perilous mountains, international mountain guide Gary Scott offers sure-footed wisdom that will guide you, step by step, until you are prepared to take on any life challenge.

Path of the Pearl

Discover Your Treasures Within
Author: Mary Olsen Kelly
$16.95, hardcover

The pearl and its legendary mystical, restorative, and healing powers have ignited imaginations for centuries. *Path of the Pearl* captures the strength of this enduring symbol by using the pearl as a metaphor for personal growth. A pearl oyster, invaded by an irritant it can't expel, turns adversity into a glowing iridescent work of nature's art. This book acknowledges and celebrates the similar path shared by women, particularly in midlife.

To order or to request a catalog, contact

Beyond Words Publishing, Inc.
20827 N.W. Cornell Road, Suite 500
Hillsboro, OR 97124-9808
503-531-8700

You can also visit our Web site at *www.beyondword.com* or e-mail us at *info@beyondword.com*.

Beyond Words Publishing, Inc.

OUR CORPORATE MISSION
Inspire to Integrity

OUR DECLARED VALUES
We give to all of life as life has given us.
We honor all relationships.
Trust and stewardship are integral to fulfilling dreams.
Collaboration is essential to create miracles.
Creativity and aesthetics nourish the soul.
Unlimited thinking is fundamental.
Living your passion is vital.
Joy and humor open our hearts to growth.
It is important to remind ourselves of love.